MW01620859

Wildflowers of Pigeon Mountain

Including Lookout Mountain,
Cloudland Canyon State Park and
Chickamauga National Military Park in Northwest Georgia

Sometimes when photographing wildflowers, the unexpected happens!

Thimbleweed *Anemone virginiana* and
female **Ruby-throated Hummingbird** *Archilochus colubris*

Including Lookout Mountain, Cloudland Canyon State Park and Chickamauga National Military Park in Northwest Georgia

by

Jay Clark

Published by
Waldenhouse Publishers, Inc.
Walden, Tennessee, USA

About the cover: *Helenium flexuosum, Passiflora incarnata, Lobelia cardinalis,* and *Mertensia virginica* are pictured against the background of the southern Appalachian mountains. Flower photographs by Jay Clark. Background photograph by Charlie Stone, Waldenhouse.

Wildflowers of Pigeon Mountain Including Lookout Mountain, Cloudland Canyon State Park and Chickamauga National Military Park in Northwest Georgia

Published by Waldenhouse Publishers, Inc.
100 Clegg Street, Walden (Signal Mt.) Tennessee 37377 USA
888-222-8228 www.waldenhouse.com
Printed in China

Library of Congress Cataloging-in-Publication Data

Clark, Jay, 1947-
Wildflowers of Pigeon Mountain : including Lookout Mountain, Cloudland Canyon State Park, and Chickamauga National Military Park in northwest Georgia / by Jay Clark.
p. cm.
Summary: "Color photographs of 374 of the most commonly occurring wildflowers found in and around the tri-state area of northwest Georgia, northeast Alabama and southern Tennessee. Captions are written in layman's terms and photos are organized by color to help the amateur easily identify flowering plants, vines, shrubs, and trees by common and scientific names" --Provided by publisher.
Includes bibliographical references and index.
ISBN-13: 978-0-9761033-1-8 (alk. paper)
ISBN-10: 0-9761033-1-1 (alk. paper)
1. Wild flowers--Georgia--Pigeon Mountain (Walker County)--Identification. 2. Wild flowers--Georgia--Identification. 3. Wild flowers--Georgia--Pigeon Mountain (Walker County)--Pictorial works. 4. Wild flowers--Georgia--Pictorial works. I. Title.
QK155.C53 2005

582.13'09758'33--dc22 2005015645

DEDICATION

This book is dedicated to the memory of my mom and dad, Frances and Herman Clark. They both appreciated and loved the outdoors. Mom was an avid flower gardener and greenhouse manager and thrilled at finding a new wildflower. People came from all around to view her flower gardens and plant cultivation skills. Some said Mom could "make a rock take root and grow." Dad had the loving heart and patience to help make it all possible.

CONTENTS

ACKNOWLEDGEMENTS

Many thanks go to Susan Clark for countless hours of computer work and editing. Thanks also to Hugh Nourse and Richard Ware with the Georgia Botanical Society. Thanks to Larry Williams for his assistance, as well. Thanks to landowners on Pigeon Mountain and Lookout Mountain for access to land and permission to photograph. These include Guy Bruce, Dean Burnette, Steven McCloud, Terry Rodgers, Huell Swader and Terry Underwood. Additionally, thanks to the Georgia Department of Natural Resources, which maintains the 18,000+ acre Crockford-Pigeon Mountain Wildlife Management Area.

Special thanks to Carol and Hugh Nourse for allowing me to use their photograph of Mountain Skullcap and to Thomas Barnes for his photograph of Dutchman's Breeches.

I am particularly grateful to Dr. Gene Van Horn, Department of Biology, University of Tennessee at Chattanooga, and to Tom Patrick, Georgia Department of Natural Resources botanist, for their peer reviews of this material.

There is an old saying "stop and smell the roses". Nowadays, many of us live such a fast-paced lifestyle that we tend to ignore or never notice the natural beauty around us. We see nature's wonders only briefly on television or in a book or the movies. Yet, flowering plants are all around us – in a vacant lot, a roadside, field or woodland. Plants provide oxygen, the majority of which comes from green plants in the oceans. Plants cleanse the environment and they filter pollutants. Flowers are the reproductive organs of plants. They produce not only fruit and seed but provide a natural beauty and curiosity that many find hard to ignore.

We cannot survive without plants. They are the basis of all food chains. They have adapted to many varied habitats and some can grow in seemingly very harsh conditions. Most are easy to find and study and they will remain for a photo unlike many other forms of wildlife that tend to avoid the camera. We are fortunate in this part of the United States to have such a wide diversity of plant life. The southeastern US is the second most diverse part of the world in flora next to the tropics. The moderate climate, rainfall, latitude and geology have produced varied soil types and habitats that in turn produce an abundance of plant life. Wildflowers, like many other forms of wildlife, are good environmental indicators. The more diverse a habitat is with native plants, the healthier the habitat.

Compared to many of the wildflower books on the shelves, this book concentrates on a small target area. It can, however, be used over much of the eastern deciduous forest. The wildflower enthusiast should especially find this book helpful when observing plants of the Cumberland Plateau and Ridge and Valley regions in northwest Georgia, northeast Alabama and south-middle Tennessee. Many wildflower books cover a very broad area and the species will show considerable variation from region to region. *Wildflowers of Pigeon Mountain* contains actual color photos of specimens from this area that should be very helpful to the local wildflower enthusiast. The plants in these photos are what one will see when out for a hike in our area. Some of the plants are not native, having been introduced from other countries and escaping cultivation to grow in the wild. Some were brought over to control erosion, form a border or fence line or simply for their beauty in the flower garden. Some can be invasive and crowd out native species.

Some of the plants, native or non-native, are poisonous when ingested. Therefore, you should never taste a plant's leaves, fruits, roots, berries, etc., unless absolutely sure of correct identification and edibility. Some of the plants were used as folk remedies for medicinal purposes. Never experiment with plants as food or medicine without consulting an experienced professional. Relying on anecdotal information or incorrect identification of a species could prove dangerous to your health.

The Wildflower Preservation Act of 1973 provided four status designations used for plants protected by the Georgia Department of Natural Resources – endangered, threatened, rare or unusual. More information on Georgia's protected plants can be found in *Protected Plants of Georgia*, a free publication from the Georgia Department of Natural Resources. Digging plants or picking flowers can have a negative impact on the population and should never be done except for properly permitted research activities. There are many commercial establishments with wild plant species under cultivation that will sell the seeds or plants and offer assistance in wildflower cultivation to the home gardener. Many of these resources are available on the Internet, through garden-supply catalogs or in horticultural magazines.

Wildflowers remind us of wilderness places and can help inspire our spirit and respect for all living things. Hopefully, this book will broaden appreciation of the natural beauty and preservation of wildflowers and the plant kingdom in general.

PIGEON MOUNTAIN

This book encompasses several areas in northwest Georgia including Lookout Mountain, Cloudland Canyon State Park and Chickamauga National Military Park but concentrates on the botanical wonder known as Pigeon Mountain. Pigeon Mountain's name was derived from its use as a roosting place by the now-extinct Passenger Pigeon, *Ectopistes migratorius*. The Passenger Pigeon used to "blacken the skies" according to accounts of early settlers in the area. The last Passenger Pigeon died in the St. Louis Zoo in 1914.

Pigeon Mountain, a spur off the larger Lookout Mountain, is a part of the Cumberland Plateau trending generally northeast to southwest. The top of Pigeon Mountain was once a synclinal valley. The fossil and stratigraphic record shows that, in earlier geological time, the present-day top of the mountain was a low-lying broad swampy area with a warm tropical environment. The dip of the rock strata on the sides of Pigeon Mountain indicates that higher mountains to the east and west have since eroded away.

Pigeon, for the most part, is now capped with Pennsylvanian-age sandstone, a harder, more erosion-resistant sedimentary rock. Thus, Pigeon Mountain was formed after the surrounding higher mountains and softer rock were weathered and eroded to lower elevations. Elevations on Pigeon range from a few hundred feet near the base to 2,329 feet at High Point, its highest peak.

Pigeon Mountain is home to numerous botanical species and diverse habitats. Deep north-facing shaded ravines contain cool flowing water. Mountain hardwoods, pine and hardwood mixes, cedar glades, meadows, bogs, springs, creeks, beaver-ponds, wetlands, early successional habitat, roadsides, agricultural areas and prescribed burn areas all co-exist on this mountain to produce the many unique botanical habitats. Rich bottomland soil, limestone soils near the base and shallow sandy soils on the mountaintop also contribute to the diverse flora.

Pigeon Mountain is also home to the Shirley Miller Wildflower Trail, a protected area on the Crockford-Pigeon Mountain Wildlife Management Area. This trail contains rare and unusual plants unique to northwest Georgia and is maintained by the Georgia Department of Natural Resources. It is easily understood why wildflower enthusiasts, professional and amateur alike, are impressed with this area and return each season to photograph and document the wide variety of plants.

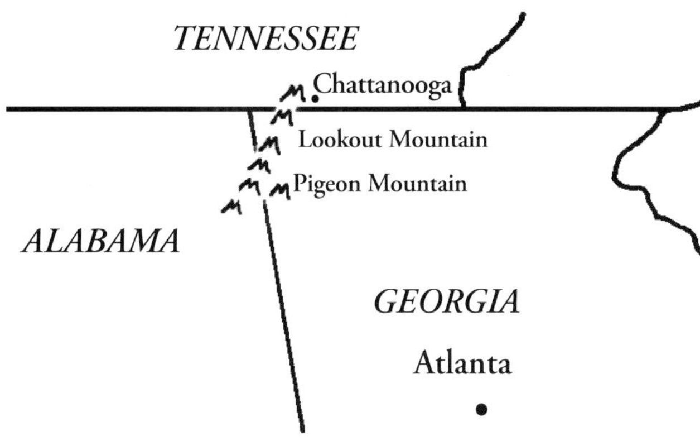

USING THE GUIDE

This book is designed to be a pictorial guide to help the amateur wildflower enthusiast with identification of certain wildflowers, shrubs, trees and vines found on Pigeon Mountain, Lookout Mountain, Cloudland Canyon State Park and Chickamauga National Military Park. It is applicable to most parts of the Eastern Deciduous Forest. The author purposefully went outside the typical 'wildflower' definition and included other plants that are wild, flowering and attract and deserve the attention of the wildflower enthusiast.

This book is not meant to be all-inclusive as no work of this size could come close to including every flowering plant; rather, it is simply a survey of the most commonly occurring showy flowering plants for the varied habitats occurring on Pigeon and Lookout mountains and Chickamauga National Military Park.

Most of us are of the picture-matching school. We look at color, shape and other characteristics and match them with a photograph. In this guide, flowers are classified by color in sections titled White Flowers, Yellow Flowers, Orange Flowers, Pink - Red Flowers, Violet - Blue Flowers and Green - Brown Flowers. To identify a plant, simply refer to the proper color section, study the photo of the plant, compare the field specimen with the photo and read its brief botanical description. Common and scientific names are given for each plant. An index is included that lists both in alphabetical order. A glossary of botanical terms and a pictorial glossary of flowers and leaves are also included.

Scientific names or binomial nomenclature originated over 300 years ago in Europe. Carolus Linnaeus (1707-1778), a Swedish botanist, perfected the modern system of taxonomic classification. This taxonomic classification includes the two-part scientific name (genus and species). The Latin language is used consistently throughout the world to avoid confusion.

Refer to the Glossary of Botanical Terms to clarify terminology. Some reference to botanical terms is essential and cannot be avoided, as this is the nature of the science. Fortunately, the reader will find that with repeated use, the terms will become a part of one's normal vocabulary. Use of scientific names is recommended when possible. However, remember that beginning wildflower enthusiasts are not familiar with these terms and, with accurate identification, the vernacular will usually suffice. The use of scientific names exclusively and refusal to use common names tends to discourage the newcomer.

Common names, however, can be confusing and should be used with caution. Many plants have more than one common name or the same common name is used for more than one species. If unsure about identification, take accurate field notes and photographs and consult a technical manual to accurately identify the species in question.

A day in the field finding and identifying just a few new plants can be very rewarding but also very overwhelming when you realize the hundreds of species that surround you. If possible, go afield with an experienced wildflower enthusiast. Join the various botanical organizations and purchase and use any of the additional field guides and technical manuals on the market. Remember that this book is only an introduction for a good day in the field. Learn a few plants at a time and before long, you will have a good start with wildflower identification.

Alabama Snow Wreath
Neviusia alabamensis has small white flowers with numerous stamens and 5 bract-like sepals. *N. alabamensis* tends to form thickets on limestone near temporary streams. The leaves are alternate, ovate to elliptic and double-toothed. This is a protected plant designated as "threatened" in the state of Georgia.

American Bladdernut
Staphylea trifolia gets its name from the inflated papery fruit capsule. Bladdernut is a shrub or small tree with opposite compound leaves and whitish, drooping clusters of bell-shaped flowers.

American Plum
Prunus americana is a shrub or small tree with shaggy bark, white flower clusters and red or yellow fruit. *P. americana* is the only wild plum with thorny twigs and sharp leaf teeth.

Aniseroot
Osmorhiza longistylis has tiny white clusters of flowers in umbels. The plant is glabrous with serrate 3-part leaves. The roots smell of anise or licorice. The specific name is derived from the style being longer than the petals. In a similar species, **Sweet Cicely,** *O. claytonia,* the style is shorter than the petals and has broader leaves.

Apple
Malus sylvestris (Malus pumila) is the common apple that escaped from cultivation. Growing in the wild it is seldom recognized. *M. sylvestris* has 5 pink-white petals and very hairy young twigs.

Balloon Vine
Cardiospermum halicacabum has tiny white 4-petaled flowers with a distinctive green inflated membranaceous seed capsule.

Bittercress
Cardamine hirsuta is an early spring plant with small white flowers. It has deeply-lobed pinnate leaves. *C. hirsuta* is found in disturbed areas and cultivated fields.

Black Locust
Robinia pseudoacacia is a tree with odd-pinnate leaves and white fragrant flower clusters in drooping racemes. There is a distinct yellow patch on the standard part of the blossom

Bloodroot
Sanguinaria canadensis is an early spring wildflower with 8 to 10 white petals and a heart-shaped leaf with 5 to 9 prominent lobes. The rootstock contains an orange-red juice.

Boneset
Eupatorium perfoliatum is easy to recognize due to the stem being enclosed with paired leaves that unite basally around the stem (perfoliate). Flowers are white, fuzzy, flat-topped clusters. Boneset is a hairy plant that likes low moist ground.

Bugbane or Black Cohosh
Cimicifuga racemosa has a slender raceme of white flowers up to 1' or more on a very tall stalk with large coarsely-toothed decompound leaves. Each flower has only a single pistil.

Bugleweed
Lycopus virginicus has very tiny 4-lobed white flowers packed into small clusters in the axils of widely-spaced pairs of elliptic, serrate leaves with a tapering petiole.

Buttonbush
Cephalanthus occidentalis is an aquatic shrub easily recognized by the white densely clustered flowers in ball-like heads.

Buttonweed
Diodia virginiana has small 4-lobed white flowers. The leaves are narrow and lanceolate. *D. virginiana* grows in wet places.

Canada Violet
Viola canadensis is a tall violet up to 20". The white petals are purple-streaked with yellow at the base. The leaves are cordate with long pointed tips and serrate margins.

Catalpa or **Catawba** or **Indian Cigar Tree**
Catalpa bignonioides is a tree with large heart-shaped leaves and clusters of showy 5-lobed white flowers. The flowers have 2 orange stripes and purple spots and stripes inside. The bell-shaped corolla is 1½" long with unequal, rounded, fringed lobes. The fruit is a bean-like pod up to 12".

Catesby's Trillium
Trillium catesbaei can be white or pink. The sepals, petals and stamen are recurved. The flower usually is nodding beneath the leaves. The bright yellow anthers are twisted outward. Grows in acid soils in dry thin woods or forest coves. Spring.

Catfoot or **Rabbit Tobacco**
Graphalium obtusifolium has both stamens and pistils in the central florets of each head. *G. obtusifolium* has lanceolate leaves, whitish-woolly beneath, and a white woolly stem. The involucral bracts are papery and whitish.

Chinese Privet
Ligustrum sinense is a tall shrub with clusters of small white bell-shaped flowers. Leaves elliptic to ovate and semi-evergreen. Branchlets and petioles pubescent. A very invasive species crowding native plant populations. Many blue-black berries.

Colic Root
Aletris farinosa has a spike-like raceme of white flowers. The flower has a swollen base and is constricted below the flaring lobes. It is rough textured with a granular appearance. Leaves are oblanceolate to narrow elliptic in a basal rosette. Meadows and upland woods. Summer.

Common Burdock
Arctium minus is similar to thistle but the leaves are not spiny. The hooked bracts form a rounded bur. The floret is lavender or white.

Common Chickweed
Stellaria media has 5 2-part white petals that are shorter than the sepals. The short ovate leaves have long stalks. The flowers are less than 1/4" wide. Chickweed likes gardens and disturbed areas.

Corn Salad
Valerianella radiata is a forked plant with opposite simple leaves and tiny 5-lobed white flowers in dense terminal heads.

Cutleaf Toothwort
Cardamine concatenata (Dentaria laciniata) has small terminal clusters of 4-petaled white flowers. The leaves are divided into 3 narrow sharply-toothed segments. Early spring.

Daisy Fleabane
Erigeron annuus has 50 or more white rays in heads 1/2" to 3/4" wide. The leaves are toothed, elliptic and sessile. Common.

Deerberry
Vaccinium stamineum is a shrub with small thin entire leaves, whitish and hairy beneath. Twigs not covered with fine 'warts' as in other plants in the *Vaccinium* genus. The flowers are white, occurring in bell-shaped clusters.

Devil's Bit
Chamaelirium luteum has staminate and pistillate flowers on separate plants. The flowers are white, dense and appear in spike-like racemes. Devil's Bit grows in rich woods. Spring.

Dewberry
Rubus flagellaris
is a prostrate plant, spreading on the ground on drier sites. Dewberry has 3- to 5-parted leaves and 5-petaled white flowers and prickles.

Dodder
Cuscuta spp. are twining vines that parasitize host plants. Dodder has yellow or orange stems with very tiny white to cream colored bell-shaped flowers. In *C. gronovii*, the ovary and capsule are not prominently beaked, as in *C. rostrata.*

Dog Fennel or **Cedarweed**
Eupatorium capillifolium is a tall densely-flowered plant with small inconspicuous flowers and clustered stems. Common in fields and pastures. Referred to as Cedarweed in north Georgia.

Downy Rattlesnake Plantain
Goodyera pubescens is notable for its basal leaves that have a network of lighter veins and a prominent white mid-vein. The flowers are white in a dense cylindrical raceme. Late spring to summer.

Dutchman's Breeches
Dicentra cucullaria has white yellow-tipped flowers drooping in a row from an arched stem. The flower has 2 spurs that resemble the upside-down 'breeches'. Early spring.

Elderberry
Sambucus canadensis grows as a small tree or large shrub. The flowers are in white clusters with purple-black berries. The leaves are opposite, pinnately-compound, with paired, elliptical, sharply saw-toothed leaflets.

English Plantain
Plantago lanceolata has all basal leaves that are narrowly elliptic to lanceolate with parallel veins. A common pest in lawns.

False Garlic
Nothoscordum bivalve has white flowers about 1" across with 6 white petals. The leaves are linear and about 1/8" wide. Spring.

False Solomon's Seal or **Solomon's Plume**
Maianthemum racemosum (Smilacina racemosa) has alternate elliptical leaves with parallel veins. The flowers are tiny, white, 6-pointed clusters at the tip of the stem. Spring.

Fireweed or **Pilewort**
Erechtites hieracifolia likes clearings and burned areas. The white disk flowers are barely visible and ray flowers are absent. The leaves are variable, toothed and alternate.

Flowering Spurge
Euphorbia corollata's flower has 5 round white bracts that surround tiny flower clusters. The flowers are in a flattened cluster arising from a small leaf whorl. The leaves are long, oval and alternate.

Fly Poison
Amianthium muscaetoxicum has a compact terminal raceme of 6-petaled white flowers on long pedicels. The leaves are long, basal and linear. The white flower turns green as it matures. Grows in grassy openings. Early summer. Lily family.

Foamflower
Tiarella cordifolia has tiny white 5-petaled flowers with 10 long stamens in a terminal raceme. Foamflower has no stem leaves. It is found in rich woods. Spring.

Foxglove Beardtongue or **Tall White Beardtongue**
Penstemon digitalis has white flowers with purple lines inside. The blossom has 5 lobes, 2 above and 3 below. The inflorescence is subtended by opposite lanceolate leaves. Found on roadsides and wood margins. Summer.

Fragrant Bedstraw or **Cleavers**
Galium asprellum has small 4-petaled white flower clusters. The leaves are mostly in whorls of sixes (some in fours and fives). The square stems are reclining with recurved prickles.

Fringetree
Chionanthus virginicus is a shrub or small tree with showy masses of white flowers. The fragrant blossoms are 1" long with a corolla of 4 narrow white lobes with purplish dots inside. The blossoms hang loosely on thin stalks in threes in drooping clusters.

Galactia
Galactia elliottii
is a trailing climbing vine in the bean family. It has white flowers that are peduncled and axillary. The leaves are compound with 7 to 9 leaflets.

Goatsbeard
Aruncus dioicus
has flowers in a branching cluster of long narrow spikes of tiny creamy-white 5-parted blossoms.

Goldenseal

Hydrastis canadensis blooms in the early spring in rich woods. It has a single terminal flower with numerous white stamens. A single large basal leaf and 2 smaller leaves are palmately-lobed and toothed. *H. canadensis* is an endangered plant in Georgia.

Great Indian Plantain

Arnoglossum muhlenbergii (Cacalia muhlenbergii) is a tall smooth plant with flat-topped clusters of white flowers. The leaves are palmately veined and lobed. The stem and leaves are not glaucous as in *A. atriplicifolia.*

Hairy Angelica

Angelica venenosa is a tall plant with white flowers that occur in umbels. The stem is slender and hairy. The leaves are compound and serrate. The petioles enlarge at the base. The upper leaves sometimes occur only as a sheath.

Hawthorn or **Fanleaf Hawthorn**
Crataegus flabellata is one of the most common hawthorns. The leaves are fan-shaped and toothed, with 4 to 6 shallow lobes. The flowers are white, 5/8" or more with 5 petals. *C. flabellata* is a shrub or small tree. *Crataegus* varies greatly and comprises a difficult genus.

Hercules Club or **Devil's Walking Stick**
Aralia spinosa is a very spiny shrub with large twice- or thrice-compound leaves. The flowers are white in flat-topped clusters.

Highbush Blueberry
Vaccinium corymbosum is a tall shrub with elliptic leaves, slightly hairy, usually without teeth. The flowers are white, small, 1/3" and urn-shaped.

Indian Hemp
Apocynum cannabinum has clusters of small greenish-white flowers terminating the main stems. The leaves are opposite and petioled. The plant has a milky latex. The corolla is cylindrical as opposed to other *Apocynum* that are bell-shaped. The branches of *A. cannabinum* overtop the inflorescence.

Indian Pipe
Monotropa uniflora is a woodland saprophytic plant 6" to 8" tall. It is waxy, translucent, white to pink in color with a single nodding flower approximately 3/4" long.

Indian Plantain
Arnoglossum atriplicifolium (Cacalia atriplicifolia) is a tall smooth plant with palmately-veined, toothed or shallow-lobed, petioled, glaucous leaves. The round stem is also glaucous. The flowers are whitish in flat-topped terminal clusters.

Japanese Honeysuckle
Lonicera japonica is an alien vine that can crowd out native species. The fragrant white or yellow flower is tube-shaped with lips. The stamens project considerably from the blossom. The leaves are opposite. The foliage is evergreen.

Jimson Weed
Datura stramonium has trumpet-shaped white or lavender-tinged flowers with 5 lobes ending in a long point. Stems are often purple and leaves coarsely toothed. All parts are poisonous.

Ladies' Tresses
Spiranthes lacera has a basal rosette of ovate leaves. The small white 1/4" flowers are spiraled in a loose terminal spike and have a greenish tinge inside.

Mandrake or **May Apple**
Podophyllum peltatum has a nodding 6 to 9 white-petaled flower in the axil of the 2 large deeply divided leaves. The fruit is yellow and edible. Spring.

Mapleleaf Viburnum
Viburnum acerifolium is a shrub with a 3-lobed serrate maple-like leaf. The leaves are hairy beneath and twigs are hairy. The flowers are white, 5-lobed, in a flat-topped cluster.

Miterwort
Mitella diphylla is named for the 2 sessile opposite leaves in the middle of the stem. The flowers are tiny, white, 5-petaled and arranged in a loose terminal spike. The petals are finely divided.

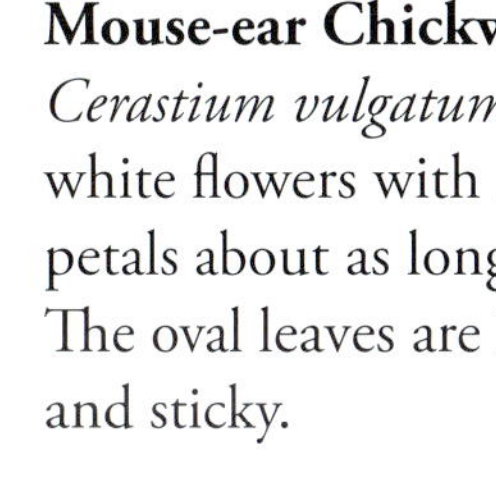

Mouse-ear Chickweed
Cerastium vulgatum has tiny white flowers with 5 deeply cleft petals about as long as sepals. The oval leaves are hairy and sticky.

Multiflora Rose
Rosa multiflora has 5 white petals. It has feather-compound leaves with 7 to 9 serrate leaflets. The leafstalks have fringed stipules. Planted for wildlife and erosion control. Can be invasive.

Narrow-leaved Mountain Mint
Pycnanthemum tenuifolium has tiny white to pinkish flower clusters less than 1/2" across. The blossoms are lobed with 2 lips. The leaves are linear, entire, 1/8" wide.

New Jersey Tea
Ceanothus americanus
is a shrub with small white flowers in oval clusters. The tiny 1/5" flowers have 5 clawed petals with 5 protruding stamens. The leaves are 3-veined, toothed, ovate and sharp-pointed.

Ox-eye Daisy
Leucanthemum vulgare
(Chrysanthemum leucanthemum)
has 15 to 30 white rays and a flat, yellow disk. The flower heads are solitary and up to 2" across. The leaves are narrow, oblanceolate and irregularly lobed. Invasive; from Europe. Commonly cultivated on roadsides.

Panicled Aster
Aster lanceolatus has its white flowers in an elongate, leafy inflorescence. The flower heads are 3/4" wide. The leaves are narrow, lanceolate, sessile and entire. Occurs in moist, low-lying places.

Partridge Berry
Mitchella repens is a creeping evergreen plant with small, paired, roundish leaves. The flower is pink or white, tubular with 4 petals. The flowers occur in pairs joined at the end of the stem.

Pennywort
Obolaria virginica has dull white to tinted purple funnel-shaped flowers with 4 pointed lobes. The opposite leaves are fleshy and purplish-green. Small plant only about 4" high. Appears in spring.

Plantain-leaved Pussytoes
Antennaria plantaginifolia has 3 round basal leaves and smaller stem leaves. The white flowers are in heads in terminal clusters. The plant leaves appear silky due to the white hair.

Poke Milkweed
Asclepias exaltata
is a tall milkweed with drooping umbels of blossoms and 5 greenish-white reflexed petals. Over this is a circle of 5 incurved horns.

Pokeweed
Phytolacca americana is a tall herbaceous plant with a red-purple stem and large entire leaves. The flowers are in racemes. The blossoms have 5 rounded greenish white to pink petaloid sepals. Young tender pokeweed is a favorite potherb in Appalachia but the mature plant can be poisonous.

Poor-man's Pepper or **Peppergrass**
Lepidium virginicum.
The leaves are alternate, toothed and stalked. Flowers are tiny, white and 4-petaled. Known more for the terminal raceme of elliptic seedpods with a slight indentation at the apex.

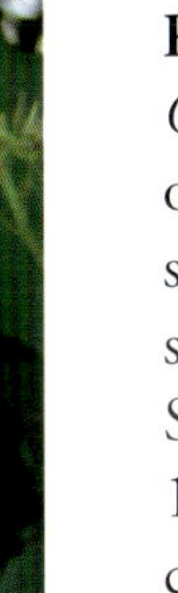

Rough-leaf Dogwood
Cornus drummondii is a shrub or small tree with elliptic sandpapery leaves on the surface, woolly beneath. Small white flowers with 1/4" petals in round-topped clusters producing white fruit in the fall.

Round-headed Bush Clover
Lespedeza capitata flowers are whitish with a pink or purple center in a dense globose cluster in the upper axils. Leaflets elliptic 1" to 1½" on short petioles.

Round-leaved Thoroughwort
Eupatorium rotundifolium has white flat-topped clusters of flowers. The leaves are short, sessile and about as broad as long; toothed and semi-clasping.

Rue Anemone
Thalictrum thalictroides (Anemonella thalictroides) has flowers with 6 to 10 white petals. The slender stalked flowers are above a whorl of small 3-lobed leaves. Blooms in early spring.

Rusty Blackhaw
Viburnum rufidulum gets its name from the rusty-colored hairs on plant parts. The leaves are elliptical with fine saw-teeth. The flowers are white with 5 rounded corolla lobes and occur in flat upright clusters.

Sericea
Lespedeza cuneata has long leafy branches. Leaflets are narrow wedge-shaped to 1" long. The white with purple flowers are grouped in the upper axils. Imported from Asia to control erosion.

Serviceberry or **Sarvis**
Amelanchier laevis has elliptical, hairless, long pointed, fine-toothed leaves that are bronzy when expanding. The flowers are white, 5-petaled in clusters. It occurs in early spring. Edible dark fruit similar to a huckleberry. Shrub or small tree.

Sharp-lobed Hepatica
Hepatica acutiloba has pointed 3-lobed leaves with hairy stalks. White flowers with 6 to 10 petals and 3 bracts underneath. Found in early spring in rich woods.

Shepherd's Purse
Capsella bursa-pastoris has tiny 4-petaled white flowers subtended by flat heart-shaped seedpods. Leaves are dandelion-like in a basal rosette.

Small-flowered Leafcup
Polymnia canadensis has variable numbers of white rays (sometimes none) less than 1/2" long with yellow disk flowers. The leaves are large, pinnately-lobed with toothed margins. The plant is hairy, sticky and has a bad odor. Prefers limestone soils.

Small White Morning Glory
Ipomea lacunosa has small white trumpet-shaped flowers with heart-shaped or 3-lobed leaves. Stem twining.

Solomon's Seal
Polygonatum biflorum is a member of the lily family. It has alternate, smooth, elliptical leaves with parallel veins. It has 2 tubular greenish-white flowers per peduncle drooping underneath the stem.

Sourwood *Oxydendrum arboreum* is a tree named for the sour lemon taste of the elliptical leaves that are yellow-green above and pale beneath. The flowers are urn-shaped, white, 5-lobed, 1/4", in terminal drooping clusters.

Star Chickweed
Stellaria pubera has 1/2" flowers with 5 white petals. The petals are almost cleft to the base making them appear to be 10 petals. The leaves are opposite, elliptic and entire. The leaves and stems are pubescent.

Star-of-Bethlehem
Ornithogalum umbellatum has 6 white elliptic petals with a green stripe underneath. The leaves are grass-like with a white midrib. The flowers bloom in early spring and form a corymb.

Starry Campion *Silene stellata* has a distinct flower with 5 white fringed petals and a bell-shaped calyx. The leaves are often in whorls of four.

Stinking Mayweed *Anthemis cotula* is a daisy-like 1" flower with a yellow disk and white notched petals. The leaves are finely dissected into threadlike segments. The plant has a fetid odor.

Swamp Dogwood *Cornus stricta* is a shrub with a broad, rounded inflorescence of tiny 4-petaled white flowers. The leaves are opposite, lanceolate to elliptic with both surfaces slightly pubescent.

Swamp Honeysuckle
Rhododendron viscosum is a fragrant white azalea. The blossom has sticky hairs on the tube and long protruding stamens. *R. viscosum* is a shrub found in moist woods.

Tickweed
Verbesina virginica has 5 or fewer white rays in its blossom. The disk flowers are also white. The leaves are lanceolate, alternate with winged petioles. The stem is also winged.

Twinleaf
Jeffersonia diphylla is an endangered species in Georgia. The 8-petaled white blossom is similar to **Bloodroot** but Twinleaf has an almost completely divided leaf on a long stalk.

Upland Boneset
Eupatorium sessilifolium has white, fuzzy, flat-topped clusters of flowers. The leaves are opposite, lanceolate, sessile and toothed.

Virgin's Bower
Clematis virginiana is a climbing plant with clusters of white 4-petaled flowers in the leaf axils. The leaves are compound with 3 coarse-toothed leaflets.

Waterleaf
Hydrophyllum canadense is an early spring, rich woods blooming plant. The flower is white to pink-purple, 3/8" long with a 5-lobed corolla and 5 long protruding stamens. The cauline leaves extend above the inflorescence and are 5- to 9- lobed.

White Baneberry
Actaea pachypoda has an oblong cluster of tiny white 4- to 10-petaled flowers with bushy stamens. Leaves are compound with serrate, lanceolate to elliptic leaflets. The berries are white with a black "eye" sometimes called a "doll's eye".

White Clover
Trifolium repens has white to slightly pink flower heads on stalks that are separate from the leaves. The leaflets are elliptic with a pale **V**-shape near the middle.

White Heath Aster
Aster pilosus has many branches and is pubescent. The flowers are 1/2" to 3/4" wide with 20 to 30 white rays and yellow to red disks. The flowered area has many small bract-like leaves. The lower leaves are linear, narrow, elliptic, entire or slightly toothed.

White Milkweed
Asclepias variegata has the typical unusual flowers of the *Asclepias* genus except that the hoods are sac-like and the horns are short. The petals are white and reflexed with a purple center. The leaves are opposite, entire and ovate. The plant has a white sap.

White Snakeroot
Ageratina altissima is a plant of the rich woods. Flowers are white and fuzzy in flat-topped clusters. Leaves are opposite, petioled, toothed and broadly lanceolate to somewhat heart-shaped.

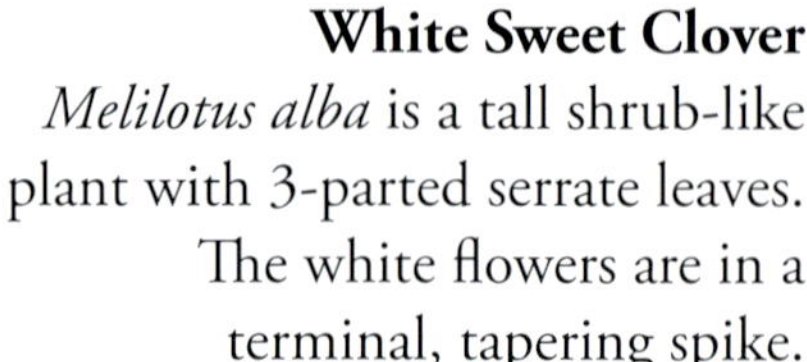

White Sweet Clover
Melilotus alba is a tall shrub-like plant with 3-parted serrate leaves. The white flowers are in a terminal, tapering spike.

White Thoroughwort
Eupatorium hyssopifolium has narrow toothed leaves arranged in whorls of 4 (or sometimes 3) with tufts of smaller leaves in the axils. The inflorescence is rounded with numerous 5-flowered heads.

White Trillium
Trillium flexipes is an early spring plant of the rich woods. It has stalked, 3-petaled white flowers, 3 greenish sepals and 3 very large, ovate, pointed, net-veined leaves.

White Vervain
Verbena urticifolia has numerous tiny white flowers on a long slender terminal spike. The leaves are opposite, toothed and elliptic.

White Wild Licorice
Galium circaezans has tiny, sparse, 4-petaled white flowers in a terminal panicle. The oval leaves are in whorls of 4 with 3 main veins.

White Wood Aster
Aster divaricatus forms sparse flat-topped clusters of few-rayed white flowers. The leaves are stalked, toothed and heart-shaped. The stem is somewhat zig-zag.

Wild Black Cherry
Prunus serotina is a tree with edible dark 3/8" cherries. The flowers are white with 5 rounded petals arranged in clusters around the ends of new leafy twigs. Leaves are elliptical and serrate.

Wild Carrot or **Queen Anne's Lace** *Daucus carota* has an umbrella-like cluster of white flowers. It is a hairy plant with 3-forked bracts and finely divided leaves. The taproot is tough and white but smells and tastes of the cultivated carrot.

Wild Hydrangea
Hydrangea cinerea is a shrub with opposite and toothed leaves that vary in shape. The leaves can be cordate, oval, elliptic or long-pointed. Fine gray pubescence on underside. The tiny white flowers form an umbrella-shaped cluster with outer layer flowers that are sterile.

Wild Potato Vine
Ipomoea pandurata
is a trailing vine with cordate entire leaves. The white bell-like flower has pink stripes radiating from the center. It is in the Morning Glory family.

Wild Stonecrop
Sedum ternatum is the common native stonecrop. The leaves are spatulate and succulent in whorls of three. The 3/8" flowers are white with 4 pointed petals in terminal cymes.

Wine Raspberry
Rubus phoenicolasius is an erect arching shrub with thorny and red-bristled stems. The leaves are greener and pubescent above, lighter beneath; compound with ovate, elliptic, pointed and serrate leaflets. Five white-pink petals. The red berry is enclosed with sepals with red gland-tipped trichomes until opening at maturity. Naturalized locally. Edible.

Wood Vetch
Vicia caroliniana has a loose raceme of 7 to 20 lavender to white 3/8" flowers with a blue-tipped keel. Compound leaves with 10 to 18 elliptic to oblong leaflets and tendrils on the end of the leaves. The stem is sprawling and sometimes purplish.

Yarrow
Achillea millefolium
has a flat-topped tight cluster of 5-rayed white flowers. The leaves are finely dissected and fern-like.

Yucca
Yucca filamentosa is a striking plant with its long, sharp-pointed basal leaves. The white flowers are bell-shaped, 6-petaled, nodding on a central stalk or panicled.

Agrimony *Agrimonia gyrosepala* has 9 or fewer primary leaflets on a principal stem leaf with slightly larger flowers than *A. parviflora.* Summer.

Angle Pod or **Climbing Milkweed** *Matelea gonocarpa* is a twining vine with cordate leaves. The flowers are yellowish-green on the outer lobes and darker in the center. The corolla lobes are more narrow and vary in color as compared to *M. carolinensis.* The flowers are stalked in clusters at the leaf axils. Blooms in late spring in moist woods and thickets.

Appalachian Golden-banner *Thermopsis mollis* has yellow pea-like flowers in terminal racemes. It has trifoliate leaves with rhombic to elliptic leaflets (hairy underneath) and narrow stipules. The stem and calyx tube also have small fine hairs. Likes dry open woods and clearings. Spring.

Appalachian Ragwort
Packera anonyma (Senecio anonymus) has yellow-rayed flowers in flat-topped clusters. The leaves are elliptical; some serrate and some deeply incised. Spring to summer.

Autumn Olive
Elaeagnus umbellata has scattered clusters of 1/4" 4-lobed creamy yellow flowers. Leaves are elliptic, alternate, silvery beneath and shiny-green above. Edible red berries preferred by wildlife. A small shrub or tree.

Bitterweed
Helenium amarum is a low plant with many linear leaves. It has yellow flowers with 5 to 10 rays. *H. amarum* is a pest and causes milk to have a bitter taste when eaten by cows. Common.

Blackeyed Susan
Rudbeckia hirta is a daisy-like flower with yellow rays and a brown disk. The stem and leaves are bristly. There is a single blossom per stem.

Blue Cohosh
Caulophyllum thalictroides has blooms in clusters of yellow-green to brown 6-pointed flowers, later replaced by deep blue berries. Each large compound leaf resembles many small leaves.

Bulbous Buttercup
Ranunculus bulbosus gets its name from the bulbous root. Five yellow petals with basal leaves in 3 segments with the end one stalked.

Bur Marigold
Bidens polylepis has yellow rays 1" or more long around a 1/2" disk. Its leaves are opposite and pinnately divided into narrow coarse-toothed segments. The seeds have barbs that attach to clothing.

Coffeeweed or **Sicklepod**
Senna obtusifolia (*Cassia obtusifolia*) has 5 yellow petals unequal in size and even-pinnately compound leaves. *S. obtusifolia* has only 2 or 3 pairs of leaflets; they are obovate and wide with the terminal leaflets larger. *S. obtusifolia* seeds remain viable in the soil for many years and once the soil is disturbed, can become very prolific.

Common Evening Primrose
Oenothera biennis has 4 broad yellow petals with a cross-shaped stigma. The sepals are reflexed. It is common on roadsides.

Common Sow Thistle
Sonchus oleraceus has yellow flower heads with many rays. The flowers average 3/4" across. The lower leaves clasp the stem with sharp-pointed lobes. Smooth bracts and stems. Waste places and fields.

Common Sunflower
Helianthus annuus is the native common sunflower that gave rise to the cultivated form. It has a large reddish-brown disk with many golden-yellow petals. The leaves are rough, hairy, stalked, serrate, lanceolate to cordate.

Crownbeard
Verbesina occidentalis has opposite, ovate to lance-ovate, serrate leaves with winged petioles. The stem is 4-winged. The flowers are yellow with 5 or fewer drooping rays. The plant is tall and grows in large colonies in fields.

Dandelion
Taraxacum officinale is probably our best-known wild plant. It spreads in the wind by the familiar white bristles attached to the seeds. Common lawn pest.

Dwarf Cinquefoil
Potentilla canadensis has 5 yellow petals and 5-parted leaves. The leaves of *P canadensis* are wedge-shaped with teeth on the rounded outer margin and a hairy stem.

Dwarf Dandelion
Krigia virginica has yellow rays 1/4" long with basal leaves deeply cut. There can be one to several of the yellow dandelion-like flowers per plant.

Dwarf St. John's Wort

Hypericum mutilum grows in wet soil. The yellow flowers have 5 petals and sepals and are less than 1/4" across. The leaves are ovate to elliptic, up to 1½" long and rounded at the base.

Fringed Loosestrife

Lysimachia tonsa has yellow, stalked 5-petaled flowers arising from leaf axils. The petals have a fringe or tooth at the apex. The leaves are ovate to lanceolate with a smooth petiole, not hairy as in *L. ciliata.*

Garden Coreopsis

Coreopsis tinctoria is a yellow-rayed flower in the daisy family. Easy to recognize with its reddish-purple disk and red-brown blotch at the base of the rays. The rays are toothed. The leaves are divided into linear segments.

Golden Aster or **Camphorweed**
Heterotheca camporum is a woolly-hairy plant with alternate leaves and yellow daisy-like flowers. The bracts are also woolly-hairy. Not a true aster.

Golden Ragwort
Senecio aureus has basal leaves that are long-stemmed, rounded, ovate with a chordate base and blunt teeth. The upper leaves are deeply cut. The flowers are daisy-like, yellow, with 8 to 12 rays in a 3/4" to 1" head.

Grass-leaved Golden Aster
Pityopsis graminifolia gets its name from the alternate grass-like leaves that appear silvery from the coating of long white hairs. The flower is yellow with up to 12 rays. *P. graminifolia* likes drier, sandy soils.

Gray Sunflower
Helianthus resinosus has up to 12 yellow 1½" rays and a disk up to 1". The bracts are reflexed. The stem is hairy. The leaves are lanceolate and alternate, scabrous above and velvety below.

Gray-headed Coneflower
Ratibida pinnata has long yellow reflexed rays and a longish gray disk. The leaves are deeply cut and whitish-hairy; the stem is also hairy.

Green-headed Coneflower
Rudbeckia laciniata has yellow drooping rays up to 1½" long. The disk is grayish or yellowish-green to 3/4" across. The leaves are toothed, 3- or 5-parted and deeply lobed.

Ground Cherry

Physalis angulata is a smooth plant with 5-lobed yellow flowers and bluish anthers. The yellow flower has brown blotches inside. *P. angulata* lacks the usual dark spots. The leaves have coarse irregular teeth. The fruit is a berry enclosed in a papery husk.

Hairy Lettuce

Lactuca hirsuta is a tall plant with a many yellow-flowered panicle. In *L. hirsuta,* the plant is hairy with dissected leaves that do not clasp the stem. The stem and bracts are red or purplish.

Hawksbeard

Crepis capillaris has a basal rosette of dandelion-like leaves. The upper leaves are narrow and clasp the stem with arrow-like lobes. *C. capillaris* has yellow flower heads 1/2" across.

Hoary Puccoon
Lithospermum canescens is a short, soft, hairy and leafy plant. The flowers are bright yellow with 5 lobes, to 3/8" wide, crowded into a terminal inflorescence. The leaves are alternate, narrow and toothless.

Hooked Buttercup
Ranunculus recurvatus gets its name from the hooked beaks on the achenes. It has 5 yellow petals and hairy, deeply-cut palmate leaves.

Hop Clover
Trifolium agrarium is the largest of the yellow clovers. It is an erect plant while the other hop clovers are prostrate. The yellow heads are 1/2" to 3/4" long. The leaves are compound with 3 leaflets.

Jerusalem Artichoke
Helianthus tuberosus is a tall hairy-stemmed sunflower. The upper leaves are alternate, hairy, toothed and taper to a long winged petiole; up to 20 rays to 1½" long with a disk less than 1/2" wide.

Lance-leaved Loosestrife
Lysimachia lanceolata has yellow 5-petaled flowers with a reddish center. The petals have a fringed outer edge with a tiny point. Leaves are elliptic to lanceolate, short ciliate, short petiolate to sessile. Open woods, meadows. Summer.

Large-flowered Bellwort
Uvularia grandiflora has a nodding, bell-like 6-pointed yellow flower. The leaves, whitish beneath, clasp the stem. This plant is stouter with a larger flower than *U. perfoliata.* Spring.

Large-flowered Leafcup or **Bearsfoot**
Smallanthus uvedelius (Polymnia uvedalia) has large opposite maple-like leaves with a winged petiole. The rays are yellow and number from 8 to 15; up to 3/4" long.

Maryland Golden Aster
Chrysopsis mariana has yellow daisy-like flower heads. The leaves are toothed, alternate and lanceolate. The bracts and stalks are sticky.

Meadow Parsnip
Thaspium barbinode has small, yellow flowers in umbels, usually 3 to 6 or more per stem. The leaves are compound with 3 or more serrate, ovate to lanceolate leaflets per stalk.

Moth Mullein
Verbascum blattaria has 5 yellow or white petals with a purple base. The stamens have purple hairs. The inflorescence is a terminal raceme along with button-like buds. Alternate, lanceolate, toothed or scalloped leaves.

Nits and Lice
Hypericum drummondii has very tiny 5-petaled yellow flowers, 1/8" wide, with ascending linear leaves about 1/2" long. The flowers are on short stalks in the axils. Dry fields.

Pale Jewel Weed or **Touch-Me-Not**
Impatiens pallida has irregular yellow petals with a pouch-like base and a spur to the rear. The mature seed capsules burst when touched.

Partridge Pea
Chamaecrista fasciculata (Cassia fasciculata) has 5 yellow petals unequal in size with a reddish blotch at the base. The leaves are even-pinnately compound with many narrow oblong leaflets.

Pencil Flower
Stylosanthes biflora is a bright yellow, rounded, pea-like flower usually solitary at the stem end. Compound leaves with 3 narrow lanceolate to elliptic bristle-tipped leaflets.

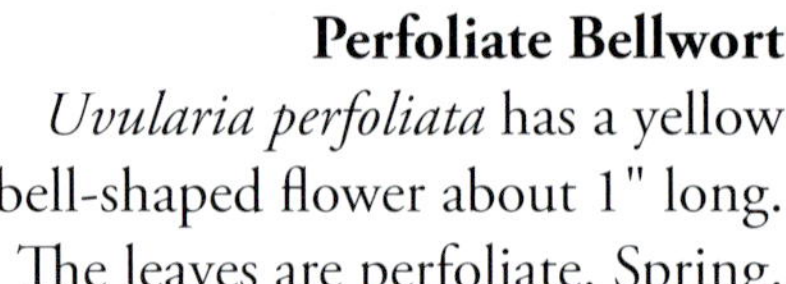

Perfoliate Bellwort
Uvularia perfoliata has a yellow bell-shaped flower about 1" long. The leaves are perfoliate. Spring.

Persimmon
Diospyros virginiana is a tree known for its sweet, orange fruit in the fall. The flowers are yellow to white, bell-shaped, with 4 lobes. Male and female on separate trees in spring. Important wildlife food.

Pineweed or **Orange-grass**
Hypericum gentianoides has many tiny 1/8" wide flowers with 5 yellow petals. The plant is many-branched into slender stems. The leaves are scale-like, appressed and very small.

Primrose Willow
Ludwigia decurrens has 3/4" wide flowers with 4 bright yellow petals. The leaves are sessile, narrow, lanceolate and extend down the stem making the stem 4-winged. Wet soils, marshes.

Purple-headed Sneezeweed
Helenium flexuosum has deflexed yellow, wedge-shaped 3-lobed rays. The disk is brown to purple and globose. The upper leaves are narrow and entire. The stem is winged down from the upper leaf.

Rough-fruited Cinquefoil
Potentilla erecta has a flattened terminal cluster of pale yellow flowers with notched petals. The leaves are compound with 5 to 7 narrow, toothed leaflets. Blooms in spring and summer in open habitats.

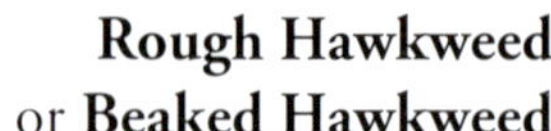

Rough Hawkweed
or **Beaked Hawkweed**
Hieracium gronovii has small yellow dandelion-like flowers. The plant is hairy with alternate elliptical leaves, smaller as they ascend the stem. Roughly cylindrical inflorescence. Seeds are beaked.

Rough Sunflower
Helianthus hirsutus has opposite, short-petioled leaves. The leaves are toothed, lanceolate, very rough on the upper surface, taper to a long point and have a rounded base. About 12 yellow rays.

Sassafras
Sassafras albidum

is an aromatic tree or shrub with variously shaped leaves (1-, 2- or 3-lobed). The yellow flowers are clustered at the end of leafless twigs. The roots and root bark contain oil of sassafras that can be used to perfume soap, make teas and tonics and to flavor root beer.

Seedbox
Ludwigia alternifolia
has 4 yellow petals and 4 conspicuous spreading sepals between the petals. The flowers occur in leaf axils. Leaves are alternate and lanceolate. Prefers moist soils.

Showy Goldenrod
Solidago speciosa has a dense inflorescence that forms a pyramidal panicle. Each head has up to 5 rays. The stem is smooth, sometimes reddish. Basal leaves are broad, elliptic, entire, with irregular edges and obscure teeth.

Small Wood Sunflower or **Small-headed Sunflower**
Helianthus microcephalus has small flowers about 1" across with only 5 to 8 rays. The stem is smooth. Leaves rough above, pale-downy beneath; lanceolate and serrate with a short 1/4" petiole.

Smooth False Foxglove or **Smooth Yellow Foxglove** or **Appalachian Oak-leach**
Aureolaria laevigata has yellow, bell-shaped 5-lobed flowers. The upper leaves are lanceolate, smooth, entire with short petioles. Lower leaves slightly lobed at the base.

Smooth Yellow Violet
Viola pensylvanica has smooth heart-shaped leaves with untoothed stipules. Stems also smooth. One to 5 basal leaves.

Spiny-leaved Sow Thistle
Sonchus asper has yellow dandelion-like flowers and prickly leaves that clasp the stem. The clasping leaf bases are conspicuously rounded.

Squawroot
Conopholis americana is a short, fleshy, scaly yellow-brown stalk with a spike of tipped and hooded yellowish flowers. It is parasitic on the roots of oak trees.

St. Andrew's Cross
Hypericum hypericoides has 4 yellow petals that form an **X**. The leaves are opposite, narrow and elliptical.

St. John's Wort
Hypericum spathulatum has 5 yellow petals with bushy stamens. The leaves are entire, paired and elliptic. This plant is shrubby with woody, 2-edged twigs.

Stonecrop
Sedum sarmentosum is a succulent plant. The 1/2" flower has 5 pointed yellow petals and occurs in a flat-topped, 3-forked inflorescence. The leaves are thick, lanceolate to 1" long.

Stoneseed or **Gromwell**
Lithospermum tuberosum has funnel-form yellow flowers with 5 lobes. The hairy leaves are oblanceolate to elliptic, clustered at the base with smaller stem leaves. *L. tuberosum* is very rare and occurs in wooded bluff habitat.

Strawberry Bush
Euonymus americanus has 1/2" yellowish, 5-petaled flowers that arise from the leaf axils on long stalks. The leaves are serrate, lanceolate to ovate. The fruit is a warty, bright red capsule.

Sundrops
Oenothera fruticosa
is one of the primroses. It has 4-petaled bright yellow flowers that open in the morning. The pods are ribbed. The leaves are lanceolate and entire. The 4-branched stigma forms a cross.

Sweet Goldenrod
Solidago odora has plume-like clusters of tiny yellow-rayed blossoms. The leaves are lanceolate, entire with parallel veins. When crushed, they smell of anise.

Tall Coreopsis or **Greater Tickseed**
Coreopsis major has yellow rays and a yellowish disk. The leaves are sessile and palmately divided into 3 narrow lanceolate leaflets and appear as a whorl of six.

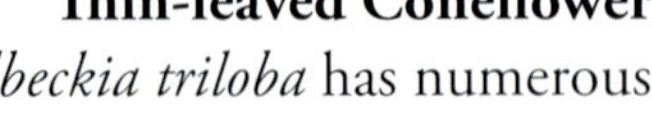

Thin-leaved Coneflower
Rudbeckia triloba has numerous radiate heads similar to *R. hirta* but smaller. The lower leaves are lobed into 3 or more segments.

Three-parted Violet
Viola tripartita has leaves with 3-part lobes or variable lobes to no lobes. The only yellow violet with dissected leaves.

Trout Lily
Erythronium americanum has 6 reflexed yellow petals, brown-purple beneath, with 2 mottled basal leaves. The fruit capsule is not indented on top as in *E. umbilicatum*. Occurs in colonies. Early spring.

Turnip or Rape
Brassica napus (Brassica rapa or *Brassica campestris)* has 1/8" to 1/2" beaks on the seed pods. The flowers are yellow and 4-petaled 1/2" wide. Leaves are lobed on the lower stem and smaller and clasping-auriculate on the upper stem.

Two-flowered Cynthia
Krigia biflora has yellow-orange dandelion-like flowers with clasping upper stem leaves. The basal leaves vary from toothed to lobed.

Whorled Loosestrife
Lysimachia quadrifolia has lanceolate leaves in regularly spaced whorls of 3 to 6. The 5 yellow-petaled flowers arise from the median leaf axils on long stalks. The flower is 1/2" across with a red center.

Wild Lettuce
Lactuca canadensis has variable leaves from pinnatifid to entire. The plant is smooth (not prickly), sometimes glaucous. It has many small yellow dandelion-like flowers with involucres less than 1/2" in height.

Wild Senna
Senna hebecarpa *(Cassia hebecarpa)* has pinnate leaves with up to 10 pairs of oval leaflets. The yellow pea-like flowers occur in the leaf axils and have unequal stamens with dark anthers.

Wild Sensitive Plant
Chamaecrista nictitans *(Cassia nictitans)* is a small plant with pinnate leaves and oval leaflets. The tiny 1/4" 5-petaled yellow flowers occur singly in the leaf axils. *C. nictitans* is sensitive to touch.

Wild Yam
Dioscorea villosa is a twining vine with long-pointed cordate leaves with prominent parallel veins. The flowers are tiny, yellow to green, 5-petaled with male and female flowers on separate plants.

Witch Hazel
Hamamelis virginiana is a shrub or small tree with wavy-edged uneven-based leaves. The flowers have 4 thin, yellow, twisted petals. The fruit (pictured) is a greenish -brown elliptical capsule with 4 curved points. The aromatic extract is used as an astringent.

Wood Betony
Pedicularis canadensis has a terminal whorl of tubular, hooded yellow to red flowers. The plant is low, hairy, with deeply incised and toothed leaves sometimes appearing reddish.

Wood Poppy
Stylophorum diphyllum has a 2" wide flower with 4 broad, overlapping yellow petals. This plant usually has only a few flowers per plant, often only one. The leaves are pinnately divided with irregular lobes. Moist, spring woods.

Woolly Mullein
Verbascum thapsus flowers have 5 yellow corolla lobes; the lower ones slightly larger. *V. thapsus* is a tall rigid plant with the flowers in a terminal spike. Another name is **Flannel Plant** for the dense covering of hairs.

Yellow Buckeye
Aesculus octandra is a tree with upright clusters of showy yellow flowers. The flower has 4 unequal yellow petals. The leaves are palmately compound. The fruit capsule produces large shiny brown poisonous seeds that at one time were used as good-luck charms.

Yellow Cress
Rorippa islandica is usually found in moist habitats. The 1/8" flowers have 4 tiny yellow petals. The leaves are lobed and coarsely toothed. Short seedpods, less than 1/4" long.

Yellow False Foxglove or **Pale Yellow Foxglove** or **Smooth Oak-leach**
Aureolaria flava has 5 lobed yellow flowers. The stems are glaucous with lanceolate upper leaves and deeply-lobed lower leaves.

Yellow Stargrass
Hypoxis hirsuta has a yellow 6-pointed 3/4" flower. The leaves are parallel veined, hairy and taller than the flower.

Yellow Sweet Clover
Melilotus officinalis has tapering, slender racemes of yellow 1/4" long flowers. The leaves are compound with 3 narrow elliptic to oblong, finely-toothed leaflets. Grows up to 5' tall.

Yellow Thistle
Cirsium horridulum is a stout plant with a yellow flower head 2" or more across with narrow spiny bracts. The leaves are pinnate and very spiny. The flower head can sometimes be purple or white.

Yellow Toadshade
Trillium luteum has a sessile flower with 3 yellow lanceolate petals and a greenish ovary, 3 green sepals and 3 broad, mottled leaves on an erect stem.

Yellow Wood Sorrel
Oxalis europaea has 5 yellow-petaled flowers with seedpod stalks not deflexed. The plant is erect with 3 obcordate leaflets per leaf.

Zig-Zag Goldenrod

Solidago flexicaulis is named for the zig-zag stem. It has broad, pointed, serrate leaves. The tiny 3- to 4-rayed yellow flowers occur in clusters in the upper leaf axils and terminally.

Butterfly Weed
Asclepias tuberosa is a common bright-orange milkweed with 5 reflexed petals and 5 erect hoods that alternate with the petals.

Carolina Lily
Lilium michauxii has 1 to 3 flowers with strongly recurved orange-red petals and protruding stamens. The leaves are arranged in whorls.

Common Orange Day Lily
Hemerocallis fulva has 6 orange petals facing upward. The blossom is not spotted as some orange lilies. *H. fulva* is a common escape from gardens.

Flame Azalea
Rhododendron calendulaceum is a mountain shrub with bright orange hairy-tubed blossoms and 5 lobes. The leaves are downy underneath.

Spotted Jewel Weed
Impatiens capensis is orange with reddish-brown spots. The funnel-shaped flower is lipped and has a spur. Mature seedpods burst open when touched; thus it is sometimes called **Touch-Me-Not.** Leaves are elliptical to lanceolate and crenate.

Trumpet Vine or **Trumpet Creeper**
Campsis radicans has trumpet-like, reddish-orange, 5-lobed flowers to 3". Compound leaves with 7 to 11 toothed lanceolate leaflets.

Yellow-Fringed Orchid
Plantanthera ciliaris is sometimes called **Orange-Fringed Orchid**. The flowers occur in a cylindrical raceme about 2" in diameter. The lip is deeply fringed. Moist fields and bogs.

American Beautyberry
Callicarpa americana is easily identified with its 5-lobed pinkish flowers arranged in axillary cymes. *C. americana* is a shrub that has lavender to purple berries in the fall.

Austrian Winter Pea
Pisum sativum is likely an escape from cultivation. It has rose-colored flowers with dark purple wings. It is a climbing vine with terminal tendrils.

Bristly Locust
Robinia hispida is a shrub legume with bristly hairs on the twigs. It has rose-colored flowers and odd-pinnate leaves. The flowers are racemes on the current season's growth. Bristly Locust is in the *Fabaceae* or bean family.

Bull Thistle
Cirsium vulgare is the only thistle in this area in which the leaf bases extend down the stem forming prickly wings. The involucral bracts have long sharp spines.

Camphorweed
Pluchea camphorata is a strong-scented plant with alternate, toothed, lanceolate to ovate leaves. It has a flat-topped inflorescence of pink flowers. *P. camphorata* grows in damp soils.

Cardinal Flower
Lobelia cardinalis is the only bright red Lobelia in the southern mountains. The red blossom has two small upper petals and three larger lower petals. The blossoms occur in a terminal spike. *L. cardinalis* prefers wet places.

Carolina Cranesbill
Geranium carolinianum is a common plant of dry disturbed sites. It has pale pink to almost white flowers with 5 notched petals about 3/8" long. The leaves are deeply cleft.

Carolina Phlox
Phlox carolina has pink blossoms with a narrow tube that ends in 5 flaring lobes. *P. carolina* has opposite, lanceolate, entire leaves. The stem is erect with the flowers in a cymose cluster at the top.

Catawba Rhododendron
Rhododendron catawbiense is a showy flowering shrub with 5-petaled pink or pale purple clustered blossoms. This shrub prefers cool moist mountain areas, usually near water.

Columbine
Aquilegia canadensis appears as red and yellow drooping bells with 5 long curved spurs. The leaves are compound, divided and subdivided into threes. *A. canadensis* likes rocky woods.

Creeping Bush Clover
Lespedeza repens is a trailing vine with smooth stem and smooth clover-like leaves and erect flowering branches arising from the leaf axils.

Crimson Clover
Trifolium incarnatum has dense, crimson, ovoid to cylindrical heads to 3" long. *T. incarnatum* is a forage plant that sometimes escapes cultivation.

Cross Vine
Bignonia capreolata gets its name from the cross-shaped pith. The plant is a woody vine. The numerous flowers are tubular with 5 lobes, dull red outside and yellow inside. The leaves are in opposite pairs each with 2 entire leaflets.

Crown Vetch
Coronilla varia has 1/2" pink flowers in long-stalked umbels. The leaves are odd-pinnate with 9 to many oblong leaflets. *C. varia* was planted to control erosion and has escaped to the wild.

Cumberland Rose Gentian or **Upland Sabatia**
Sabatia capitata is many-petaled with sessile pink to lavender flowers. Basal and stem leaves similar. Rare but does occur in northwest Georgia and is a protected plant. Prefers mowed roadsides.

Dense Blazing Star or **Blazing Star** *Liatris spicata* has pink sessile flowers in a crowded terminal spike. The stem leaves are grass-like and linear. The bracts are blunt and often purplish. Moist meadows. Summer.

Deptford Pink
Dianthus armeria is a small 5-petaled pink flower 1/2" wide with white dots and a few teeth on the petals. The leaves are very narrow and ascending.

Diodia or **Rough Buttonweed** or **Poor-Joe**
Diodia teres is a low plant with linear, sessile, paired leaves. The 1/4" long flower is pink, 4-lobed, and funnelform in the leaf axils.

Everlasting Pea
Lathyrus latifolius has pink, purple or white pea-like blossoms. Stems are winged. The leaves have a pair of blades and a terminal tendril.

Field Thistle
Cirsium discolor is a tall thistle up to 6' in height with smooth stems and leaves white-woolly beneath. The flowers are purplish-pink; up to 2" long. Just below the flowers are narrow ascending leaves.

Fire Pink
Silene virginica has 5 bright red petals, notched at the tip. The calyx is tubed and sticky to the touch. The flowers have a long stalk. The leaves are paired and opposite.

Flowering Dogwood
Cornus florida is a small flowering tree, one of the most showy early spring plants. In some areas, *C. florida* is being devastated by an anthracnose fungus disease.

Fog Fruit or **Frogfruit**
Phyla lanceolata has globose heads with tiny 4-lobed, pink flowers on a stalk above the leaves. The leaves are lanceolate and serrate except near the base. Found in wet areas.

Hedge Nettle *Stachys latidens* has a spike of pink flowers with an upper inverted cup that covers the 4 stamens. The lobes have darker pink irregular lines. The lower lobes are bent sharply downward. Stems are pubescent on the angles. Leaves are opposite, petioled, serrate-crenate, lanceolate to elliptic and rounded to cordate at the base. Moist woods, low meadows. Summer. Mint family.

Himalaya Berry
Rubus bifrons is the only completely pink-flowered blackberry in our area. All other species of *Rubus* have white flowers.

Hoary Mountain Mint
Pycanthemum incanum is easy to identify due to the upper leaves appearing white and powdery. The pinkish flower heads occur terminally or secondary in the axils.

Horse Gentian
Triosteum perfoliatum has large connate-perfoliate entire leaves near the middle of the stem. The stem and leaves are hairy. Flowers are purplish-red with 5 erect lobes growing sessile in the leaf axils. Grows in open woods and clearings. Blooms in late spring. Sometimes called **Tinkerweed** or **Wild Coffee**.

Indian Pink
Spigelia marilandica has a distinct crimson tubular flower 1" to 1½" long, yellow on the inside. The 5 lobes of the corolla form a yellow star at the top of the blossom. Grows in rich woods. Late spring to early summer.

Joe-Pye Weed
Eupatorium fistulosum has pinkish-purple flowers in a domed cluster. The glaucous stem is smooth, tinged with purple and hollow in cross section. The 4 to 7 whorled lanceolate leaves are blunt-toothed. Creek banks, moist soils.

Meadow Beauty or
Virginia Meadow Beauty
Rhexia virginica has 4 deep-pink petals and slender curved anthers. The leaves are opposite, ovate and wider at the base than the similar *R. mariana.* The stem is square with 'wings' or ridges running length-wise.

Moss Phlox
Phlox subulata has pink to lavender 5-petaled, notched flowers. The leaves are thin and needlelike. *P. subulata* grows in creeping mats. Escape from cultivation.

Mountain Laurel
Kalmia latifolia is a showy evergreen shrub with pink-white flower clusters. The cup-shaped blossoms have 5 pointed lobes and 10 stamens. The leaves are shiny, alternate and elliptic with a yellow-green petiole.

Narrowleaf Trillium
Trillium lancefolium has maroon petals and down-turned green sepals. The mottled leaves are narrow and elliptic to lanceolate.

Pink Azalea
Rhododendron nudiflorum is a shrub with 5-lobed pink tubular flowers and long, protruding stamens. The blossom occurs with or before the leaves.

Pink Lady's Slipper or **Moccasin Flower** *Cypripedium acaule* is a member of the orchid family. It has 2 basal leaves with parallel venation and a single flower. Two of the petals are greenish and the 3rd is pink and shaped like a moccasin or slipper. Found in acid soils of pine woods or pine-hardwood mix. It is designated as an "unusual" plant in Georgia and is protected.

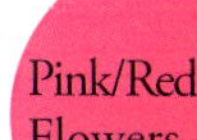

Pink Smartweed
Polygonum pensylvanicum has cylindrical, terminal, tight racemes of tiny light pink to white flowers. The leaf joints are swollen with a distinctive fringeless sheath (ocrea) that surrounds the stem at the leaf point.

Pink Wild Bean
Strophostyles umbellata has pink, pea-like flowers on stalks that exceed the leaves. The leaves are compound with 3 narrow lanceolate leaflets. The standard is rounded and the keel is curved upward.

Pointed-leaved Tick Trefoil
Desmodium glutinosum has leaves in a whorl at the tip of a short stem. From this whorl of pointed ovate leaves is a single slender flower stalk with a terminal panicle of pink to lavender pea-like blossoms that produce a greenish jointed seedpod.

Red Buckeye
Aesculus pavia is a shrub or small tree with opposite fan-compound leaves and 5 elliptic leaflets. The showy clusters of flowers are bright red and tubular with the stamens inside the tube.

Red Clover
Trifolium pratense is one of the most common clovers. It is actually rose to lavender in color. Leaflets are elliptic with a lighter area in their centers.

Redbud or **Judas Tree**
Cercis canadensis is a small tree with showy pinkish to red spring flowers that appear before the leaves. The leaves are smooth, entire and distinctly cordate.

Rose Pink
Sabatia angularis has a thick 4-angled winged stem. Opposite upper branches and sessile leaves. Five pink petals with a yellow star-shaped eye. Moist areas.

Rosebay Rhododendron
Rhododendron maximum is a large flowering shrub. The blossom has 5 pink petals sometimes spotted with green or orange. Leaves are lanceolate, large and leathery. Moist mountain woods and streambanks.

Sensitive Briar
Schrankia microphylla is a sprawling plant with prickly thorns. Leaves are bipinnately compound with many segments that 'fold' when touched. The rose-pink flowers form a rounded head.

Showy Evening Primrose
Oenothera speciosa has 4 pink overlapping petals with darker pink streaks and a yellow center. Petals are sometimes white. The leaves are elliptic, blunt-toothed or lobed. Found on roadsides and fields.

Showy Orchis
Galeorchis spectabilis *(Orchis spectabilis)* has 1" flowers. The purple to rose-colored sepals and lateral petals form a rounded hood. The lip is white and points downward. The 2 basal leaves are elliptic and smooth. Rich woods.

Silktree or **Mimosa**
Albizia julibrissin is a small tree with a flattened crown and showy pink flower clusters. The flowers have long thread-like pink stamens, whitish at the base, crowded into a stalked ball-like cluster. The leaves are bipinnately compound and fern-like.

Small-leaved Mint
Mentha cardiaca has pink flowers in dense whorls in the upper axils along with smaller leaves than the ordinary foliage leaves. The leaves are petioled, elliptic and serrate, often purplish to reddish.

Small Red Morning Glory
Ipomea coccinea has scarlet, trumpet-shaped flowers and heart-shaped leaves. The flower is about 2/3" across. The stem is twining.

Spotted Wintergreen
Chimaphila maculata has pinkish to white 5-petaled, nodding flowers. The leaves are 3-whorled, lanceolate, toothed, with a lighter mid-vein pattern.

Spring Beauty
Claytonia caroliniana has 5 white to pink petals with darker pink veins. The leaves are oblanceolate, wider than *C. virginica.*

Sweet Shrub
Calycanthus floridus has fragrant maroon petals and sepals that smell like strawberries when crushed. The leaves are long, pointed, opposite, elliptic and hairy underneath. Spring.

Tall Thistle
Cirsium altissimum has pink flower heads. The stem leaves are lanceolate and mostly unlobed but may have some teeth. Leaf undersides are whitish-woolly.

Toadshade
Trillium cuneatum
has leaves, petals and sepals in whorls of 3, as do all Trilliums. The stalkless flower has erect maroon or purplish petals and spreading sepals.

Trailing Arbutus
Epigaea repens has pink or white flowers with 5 flaring lobes. The leaves are oval and leathery. The stems are hairy and trailing. A low, creeping plant.

Wild Basil
Satureja vulgaris is a hairy plant with pointed, oval, slightly toothed, opposite leaves. The inflorescence is a compact terminal cluster of 1/2" long pink to lavender flowers with bristly bracts. Occasionally, the flowers occur in the upper leaf axils.

Wild Bean
Phaseolus polystachios has pinkish-purple flowers in a loose raceme on a long stalk. The 2-sided leaflets are asymmetrical. The plant is a twining vine and produces a curved seedpod.

Wild Garlic

Allium canadense has tiny 6-petaled pale pink flowers on short stalks. Bulblets may replace or be mixed with flowers. The flattened, narrow, grass-like leaves are mostly basal.

VIOLET/BLUE FLOWERS

Arrow-leaved Aster
Aster sagittifolius has blue to violet rays with many tiny leafy bracts on the flowering branches. The lower leaves are lanceolate to elliptic, narrowing into long, winged stalks. Fall.

Bicolor Lespedeza
Lespedeza bicolor is a legume shrub with a terminal inflorescence of rosy purple flowers. It is often used as a wildlife food.

Bird's-eye Speedwell
Veronica persica is a decumbent, pubescent annual. The ovate leaves are opposite, crenate-dentate, becoming crowded, alternate and smaller as they ascend the stem. The 1/2" blue flower has 4 petals with darker blue veins and a white center.

Birdsfoot Violet
Viola pedata has finely-divided leaves with 9 to 15 points. *V. pedata* has 5 petals, the lowest wider with marked veins.

Blue Lettuce
Lactuca villosa is a tall leafy plant with many small blue daisy-like flowers. This variety has serrated, lanceolate, unlobed leaves.

Blue Toadflax
Linaria canadensis has lavender to white flowers less than 1/2" long arranged in a terminal raceme. The leaves are short and linear, usually below the middle of the plant.

Blue-eyed Grass
Sisyrinchium augustifolium has 6 blue petals each tipped with a small point. It has flat stems with grass-like leaves less than 1/4" wide.

Bluestar or **Blue Dogbane**
Amsonia tabernaemontana has a rounded cluster of flowers with 5 blue petals. The leaves are lanceolate, alternate and close together on the stem.

Bluet
Houstonia caerulea has small 1/2" 4-petaled flowers, pale blue to white with a yellow eye. The stem leaves are paired, short and narrow. Basal leaves are spatulate.

Bushy Aster
Aster dumosus, at flowering time, has a great many short, bract-like leaves. It is a multi-branched plant with pale blue flowers of about 20 rays. The heads are 1/2" to 3/4" wide. Fall.

Butterfly Pea
Clitoria mariana is a twining vine with pinkish-lavender flowers. It is in the bean family. The leaves are pinnately compound.

Caley Pea or **Singletary Pea**
Lathyrus hirsutus has a pea-like flower with blue to violet petals. The stems are sprawling and 2-winged. The leaves have 2 leaflets with tendrils and winged petioles. The racemes have 1 to 4 flowers on nodding pedicels. The seedpod is densely hirsute. Fields and waste places. Late spring.

Climbing Milkweed
Matelea carolinensis is a twining vine with cordate leaves. The flowers are brownish-purple, 3/4" wide with 5 spreading lobes. The flowers are stalked in clusters in leaf axils. Blooms in late spring in moist woods or thickets.

Common Blue Violet
Viola sororia is our most widespread and easily recognized violet. It has smooth heart-shaped leaves, blue to violet flowers with a white center and 5 unequal petals.

Common Milkweed
Asclepias syriaca has thick, wide, elliptic, petioled leaves. The rose to purple flowers are crowded in rounded umbels, often nodding. Distinguished by fragrant flowers and warty seedpods.

Crested Dwarf Iris
Iris cristata is a small blue iris only a few inches in height. The down-curved sepals have a yellow crest. The leaves are short and embrace the stem. Spring.

Cross-leaved Milkwort
Polygala cruciata has dense flower heads in cylindrical racemes. The color varies from pinkish-lavender to greenish-white. The narrow leaves are in whorls of 4 forming a cross. Moist habitats. Summer to fall.

Curtiss' Milkwort
Polygala curtissii has lavender to rose colored flowers in dense heads on single stems. The leaves are alternate and narrow. Open woods and fields. The blossom reminds one of a clover blossom but is pointed in early growth.

Dayflower
Commelina communis is a succulent plant with 2 larger upper blue petals and a smaller lower white petal. This species was introduced from Asia.

Downy Lobelia
Lobelia puberula has blue to lavender flowers with 2 narrow lobes above and 3 wider lobes below. The leaves are alternate, finely downy, ovate and toothed. The inflorescence is usually to one side of the stem and terminal. Open clearings. Summer.

Downy Wood Mint
Blephilia ciliata has 1/2" flowers, lavender with purple spots. The flower clusters are rounded and crowded on the upper stem. The leaves are short-petioled to sessile and slightly toothed. Summer.

Dwarf Larkspur
Delphinium tricorne has a terminal raceme of 5-petaled blue or white spurred flowers. The leaves are deeply cleft into 5 to 7 pointed lobes.

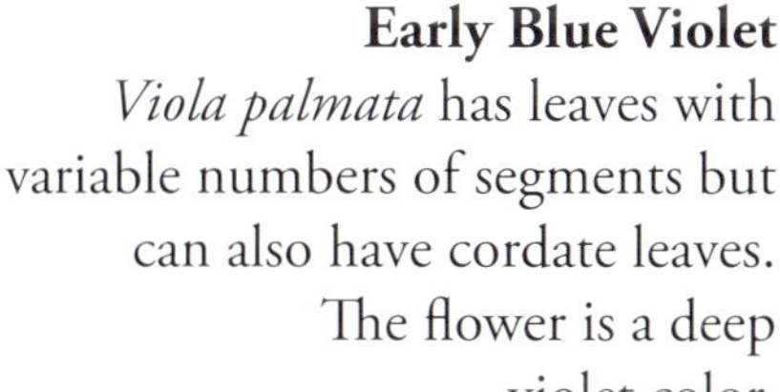

Early Blue Violet
Viola palmata has leaves with variable numbers of segments but can also have cordate leaves. The flower is a deep violet color.

Elephant's Foot
Elephantopus carolinianus is similar to *E. tomentosus* but has leaves up the stem at the base of the branches. The basal leaves are absent at flowering time.

Elephant's Foot
Elephantopus tomentosus has pale purple flowers arranged in circular 2 to 5 flowered heads with leaf-like bracts. In *E. tomentosus,* the leaves are mostly basal and lie flat on the ground.

Field Madder
Sherardia arvensis is a dense bedstraw-like plant, low to the ground, with tiny leaves in whorls of 4 to 6. The flowers are blue to pink with a slender tube and 4 spreading lobes. The flowers are in terminal heads.

Garden Larkspur
Consolida ambigua (Delphinium ajacis) has blue, white or pink flowers with 1 spur and 2 fused petals. The plant is easy to identify with its deeply dissected leaves with linear segments. This European annual is found on roadsides and waste places, blooming in late spring or summer.

Geranium
Geranium maculatum has 5 rose to purple petals with a distinct beak in the center of the flower. The leaves are toothed and deeply 5-parted.

Groundnut
Apios americana is a climbing vine with pinnate leaves with 5 to 7 leaflets that taper to a sharp point. The flowers are 1/2" long and fragrant with brownish-purple to brownish-pink petals. They occur in dense racemes in the axils. *A. americana* grows in moist bottomland.

Hairy Skullcap
Scutellaria elliptica has a blue to violet corolla in branching racemes near the summit. Hairy stems and leaves. The leaves are crenate, elliptic to rhombic-ovate with leaf tissue down the petiole. Deciduous woods and roadside banks. May to June.
Mint family.

Heal-All or **Self Heal**
Prunella vulgaris is a small mint-like plant with a terminal, cylindrical spike of violet flowers up to 5/8" long. The upper lip is hood-like and the lower lip is bent downward with a fringed median lobe.

Heart-leaved Aster
Aster cordifolius is a pale blue to pale violet or white aster with cordate, serrate leaves with deep notches at the base. The flower heads are in dense clusters with the disk turning reddish. Late summer to fall.

Heart-leaved Skullcap
Scutellaria ovata has a blue to violet corolla 1/2" to 3/4" long. The leaves and stems are hairy. The leaves have crenate margins, long petioles and are ovate to ovate-lanceolate with cordate bases.

Henbit
Lamium amplexicaule
has rounded, scalloped leaves, the upper ones sessile or clasping. The purplish-lipped flowers occur in the leaf axils. *L. amplexicaule* is a member of the mint family and occurs on waste ground.

Hog Peanut
Amphicarpa bracteata is a twining vine in the pea family. The leaves are compound with 3 pointed leaflets. The flowers are lilac and occur in drooping clusters in the leaf axils.

Violet/ Blue Flowers

Horse Nettle
Solanum carolinense has blue to violet flowers with 5 lobes. The stem is prickly; the leaves widely toothed. The fruit is an orange-yellow berry.

Ivy-leaved Morning Glory
Ipomoea hederacea has 3-lobed leaves and hairy long-pointed sepals. The flowers are trumpet-like and usually blue to purple but can be white or pink. Sometimes considered a garden pest.

Kudzu
Pueraria lobata is a spreading vine, brought from Japan to control erosion. The leaves are trifoliate. The flowers are violet to purple in dense clusters with a grape-like fragrance. Can be invasive and a pest.

Late Purple Aster
Aster patens has entire leaves with rounded lobes that nearly encircle the hairy stem. The blue to violet heads are about 1" across with yellow or reddish disk flowers. Fall.

Long-leaved Bluet
Houstonia longifolia has terminal clusters of flowers in twos or threes. White to lavender flowers with slender paired leaves.

Long-spurred Violet
Viola rostrata is a leafy-stemmed violet with a distinctive spur 1/2"or more in length behind the petals. The flower is blue to violet; leaves are heart-shaped and pointed.

Lowrie's Aster
Aster lowrieanus has pale blue to white blossoms in open panicles or erect racemes. The leaves are smooth and vary from cordate to lanceolate with flat, winged petioles. Fall.

Lyre-leaf Sage
Salvia lyrata has a basal rosette of irregularly cleft leaves. The stem is square with small, paired leaves. The flowers are blue to violet in a loose terminal spike.

Mad-dog Skullcap
Scutellaria lateriflora has the smallest flowers of the skullcaps. The tiny 1/4" flowers are in 1-sided racemes in the leaf axils. The leaves are opposite, toothed, ovate to ovate-lanceolate. Swamps and alluvial woods. Summer. Early settlers thought it to be a remedy for rabies.

Mistflower
Conoclinium coelestinum (Eupatorium coelestinum) has bluish, fuzzy, flat-topped clusters of flowers. The leaves are triangular, blunt-toothed, stalked and opposite.

Mountain Skullcap
Scutellaria montana has a 4-sided stem covered with soft, knob-tipped hair. The hairy, opposite leaves are elliptic to ovate and have serrate or crenate margins. The flowers are in terminal racemes. The corolla lobes are pale-blue at the tip and white at the base. *S. montana* is a threatened species at both state and federal levels.

Narrow-leaved Vervain
Verbena simplex has spikes of lavender or purple flowers with opposite, narrow, lanceolate, toothed leaves that taper to a stalkless base.

New York Ironweed
Vernonia noveboracensis is a tall plant with deep purple to violet flowers in a flat-topped inflorescence. The leaves are narrow, lanceolate and alternate. The involucral bracts taper to a narrow tip. Moist open areas.

Pale Meadow Beauty
Rhexia mariana has 4 pale lavender to pink petals with long, curved yellow anthers. The stem is hairy and the leaves opposite. Found in damp sandy soils.

Panicled Tick Trefoil
Desmodium paniculatum is different from other trefoils in that it has narrow leaflets, lanceolate to linear with long petioles. The flowers are purplish to pinkish, less than 1/2" long. The fruits have tiny hooked hairs that stick to clothing. Sometimes called **Sticktight.**

Passion Flower or **Maypop**
Passiflora incarnata is easily identified by the unusual flower structure: 5 sepals, 5 petals, a fringe-like corona and 3 spreading styles. *P. incarnata* is a trailing vine with lobed leaves and edible fruit. Tennessee state wildflower.

Periwinkle
Vinca minor has 5 blue to violet asymmetric petals that create a pinwheel appearance. It has opposite, shiny evergreen leaves. Brought from Europe, it has escaped cultivation and often grows wild in the woods.

Petunia
Ruellia caroliniensis has a lavender to blue trumpet-shaped flower with 5 flaring lobes. Flowers occur in sessile clusters in the upper leaf axils. The plant is hairy with opposite elliptic leaves.

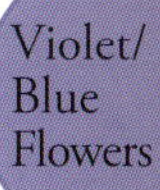

Polygala
Polygala verticillata has linear leaves in whorls of 3 to 6 on the lower stem. The flowers are tiny, pale lavender to pale pink, in short tapering racemes on a long stalk.

Purple Bluet or
Large Houstonia

Houstonia purpurea has flowers in terminal clusters. Blossoms are tubular with 4 flaring lobes; pale lavender to white. Leaves are opposite, sessile, entire, oval and 3-veined.

Purple Dead Nettle

Lamium purpureum has pink to purple lipped flowers in a leafy spike. The ovate purplish leaves tend to overlap. *L. purpureum* is in the mint family. Found in waste places and disturbed areas.

Purple Phacelia

Phacelia bipinnatifida has violet to blue flowers 1/2" broad, bell-shaped, with 5 lobes and protruding stamens. The plant is hairy with long-petioled, bipinnately divided stem leaves.

Robin's Plantain
Erigeron pulchellus has 50 to 100 pale lilac to violet rays. The heads are about 1" across. The plant is hairy with scalloped basal leaves. This species has fewer rays and larger but fewer heads than **Common Fleabane.**

Sainfoin
Psoralea onobrychis has a blue-violet spike of small pea-like flowers that usually do not rise above the foliage. The leaves are compound with 3 ovate leaflets up to 4" long. Open woods and fields. Summer. Pea family.

Sampson's Snakeroot
Psoralea psoralioides has compound leaves with 3 lanceolate to elliptic leaflets. The flowers are blue to purple, 1/4" long, in slender racemes usually above the leaves.

Sharp-winged Monkey Flower
Mimulus alatus has violet to pink lipped, tubed flowers on short stalks in the leaf axils. The leaves are lanceolate, stalked, toothed and opposite. Found in swamps.

Smooth Vetch
Vicia dasycarpa, a member of the bean family, has 10 to 30 purple to lavender flowers in a raceme. The terminal leaflet is modified into a tendril. A sprawling vine.

Southern Harebell
Campanula divaricata has 1/8" blue to lavender bell-shaped flowers nodding on panicled, horizontal branchlets. The lobes are recurved and the style protrudes beyond the corolla. Leaves are toothed and lanceolate.

Spiderwort
Tradescantia virginiana has a terminal cluster of 3-petaled violet flowers with bright yellow-golden stamens. The leaves are parallel-veined and iris-like.

Spiked Lobelia
Lobelia spicata has pale blue to white flowers in a terminal spike. The leaves are obovate and slightly toothed near the base and reduced to bracts up the stem.

Spurred Butterfly Pea
Centrosema virginianum is similar to *Clitoria mariana* but the standard is more rounded. The leaves are compound with 3 leaflets. The stem is a twining vine. Open areas. Summer.

Tall Bellflower
Campanula americana does not have a bell-shaped flower. The flower is 5-lobed, flat, pale blue, with a white throat. The long style is recurved. The leaves are serrate and lanceolate.

Trailing Trillium
Trillium decumbens has purplish petals similar to *T. sessile.* The stem is decumbent, allowing the leaves to lie on the ground.

Triangle-leaved Violet or **Arrowhead Violet**
Viola sagittata *(Viola emarginata)* has narrow, triangular leaves, some basal teeth but lacks the back-flaring basal points. Blue to lavender 5-petaled flowers on a leafless stem.

Turnsole
Heliotropium indicum has its inflorescence arranged in a helical raceme with 2 rows of crowded blue to lavender flowers. Leaves are ovate to elliptic and petiolate.

Venus' Looking Glass
Specularia perfoliata has 5 spreading violet to blue lobes; not bell-like. The flowers occur solitary in the axils of roundish, clasping, toothed leaves.

Violet Wood-Sorrel
Oxalis violacea has 5 flaring lobes, rose to lavender or lavender to violet, on a bell-shaped calyx. Leaves are compound with 3 inverted heart-shaped leaflets, sometimes purplish underneath.

Virginia Bluebells
Mertensia virginica is an early spring plant of rich, moist woods. The flowers are pink in bud but change to blue. The blossoms are trumpet-like and nodding. The leaves are oval, smooth and entire with prominent veins.

Wild Bergamot
Monarda fistulosa is a member of the mint family. The plant has a square stem with opposite, serrate, petioled, lanceolate leaves. The flowers are lilac, lipped and tubular in a terminal globose cluster.

Wild Blue Phlox
Phlox divaricata is different from the other phlox species in that it is light violet to blue in color instead of pink or purplish. The corolla is 1" wide with wedge-shaped lobes, notched at the apex. The flowers occur in terminal clusters. The stem is hairy-sticky and leaves are sessile, opposite, entire and lanceolate.

Wild Hyacinth
Camassia scilloides is a member of the lily family. The flowers are 6-petaled, light blue, on short stalks in a terminal raceme. The leaves are grass-like and keeled.

Wild Onion
Allium stellatum has an umbel of 6-pointed tiny lavender flowers. The leaves are grass-like. The bulb has a strong onion odor.

Wild Pansy
Viola rafinesquii is a small delicate plant with spatulate leaves and scalloped margins. It has deeply lobed stipules. The flower is small, long stalked, white to blue, with short spurs and sepals.

Wisteria

Wisteria sinensis is a high-climbing vine in the bean family. *W. sinensis* has fragrant compact clusters of blue to violet flowers in a raceme to 12" in length. Compound leaves with 9 to 11 leaflets. The legume is velvety pubescent.

Woodland Lettuce

Lactuca floridana is a tall blue lettuce. It has from 11 to 17 1/2" blue flowers in a loose panicle. The pappus is white. The stem is sometimes reddish. The leaves are deeply lobed, dandelion-like, not clasping.

American Columbo
Frasera carolinensis is a tall plant with a pyramidal panicle of flowers. The 4 greenish-white or yellow petals have brown-purplish dots and a green gland with prominent hairs. Lanceolate leaves in whorls of 4. Limestone soils in open woods and meadows. Late spring to early summer.

Clearweed
Pilea pumila has one-sided panicles of greenish flowers in the leaf axils. The leaves are ovate, crenate, lustrous with prominent veins and slender petioles. Stout translucent stems. Marshes and moist woods. Resembles **Stinging Nettle** but lacks stinging hairs.

Curly Dock
Rumex crispus has wavy leaf margins with green to brown flowers with heart-shaped seed wings. A common plant in fields and waste places.

False Nettle
Boehmeria cylindrica has no stinging hair as in *U. dioica.* The leaves are opposite and toothed. The flowers are without petals and separate with male and female flowers on the same plant. The flowers are greenish on axillary spikes.

Ginseng
Panax quinquefolius has a pale greenish-yellow flower on a slender stalk in a round cluster in the leaf axil. The plant is low with 3 long-stalked leaves, each with 5 toothed leaflets. Produces red berries in the fall. Rich woods.

Green Dragon
Arisaema dracontium is uncommon but easily recognized by its long slender spadix extending far beyond the narrow spathe. The leaf occurs singly with several elliptical leaflets. Rich moist woods. Spring to summer. *Araceae* or *Arum* family.

Green Violet
Hybanthus concolor has small green, drooping flowers, singly from the leaf axils. Leaves are alternate, short petioled lanceolate to elliptic.

Honey Locust
Gleditsia triacanthos is a tree with compound leaves and branched thorns growing from the bark. The flowers are small, greenish and clustered. The fruit is in long flattened pods with a sweet pulp between the seeds.

Horseweed
Conyza canadensis *(Erigeron canadensis)* is a tall weed with many linear leaves and numerous flowers from the upper leaf axils. The 1/4" flowers are greenish with tiny white rays that are compressed and do not spread.

Jack-in-the-Pulpit or **Indian Turnip**
Arisaema triphyllum is a familiar plant of moist rich woodlands. The spathe is green or purplish and curves over the club-shaped spadix. The flowers are tiny at the base of the spadix. The leaves are divided into three parts on a tall stalk. The fruit is a cluster of red berries.

Little Brown Jug
Hexastylis arifolia has evergreen triangular leaves that are sometimes varigated. The purplish to olive brown flowers occur at the base of the plant and have short, tubular, 3-lobed calyxes constricted just below the 1/4" spreading lobes.

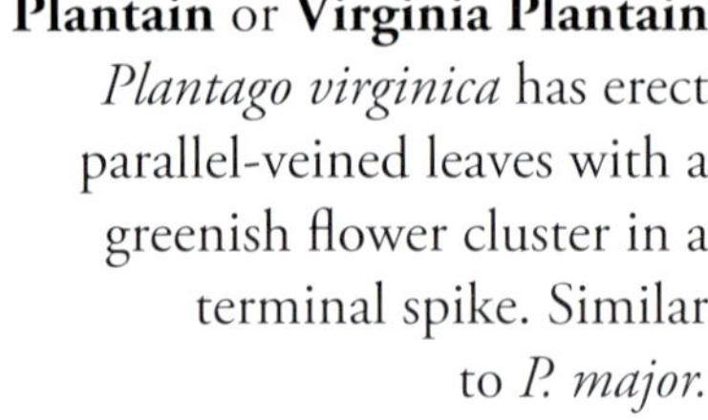

Plantain or **Virginia Plantain**
Plantago virginica has erect parallel-veined leaves with a greenish flower cluster in a terminal spike. Similar to *P. major.*

Poison Ivy
Toxicodendron radicans (Rhus radicans) is a trailing or climbing vine with tiny greenish to white flowers in axillary panicles. The leaves are compound with 3 leaflets that may be entire, toothed or shallow-lobed. A contact poison.

Ragweed
Ambrosia artemisiifolia has greenish flowers in a terminal raceme. The leaves are twice divided. The infamous pollen causes hay fever.

Spider Milkweed or **Antelope Horn**
Asclepias viridis has terminal clusters of large showy greenish-yellow flowers. The petals are spreading with ascending tips. The hoods are small and the horn is a small flat median plate. There are no deflexed lobes as in most *Asclepias.* Thin woods to prairies. Late spring. Rare.

Thimbleweed
Anemone virginiana has blossoms with 5 greenish-white sepals on the upper stem. The leaves are toothed, 3- to 5-parted. The fruit head resembles a thimble.

Thorny Pigweed
Amaranthus spinosus has long sharp-spined stipules. The green flowers are in terminal panicles. The leaves are rhombic to ovate with long petioles. A common barnyard weed.

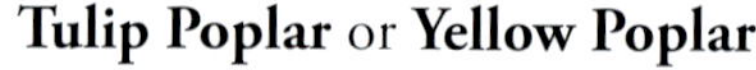

Tulip Poplar or **Yellow Poplar**
Liriodendron tulipifera is a large tree with showy tulip-like flowers. The blossom is cup-shaped with 6 greenish petals (orange at base). The leaves are an unusual shape with a recurved base and broad tip with 4 to 6 short, pointed, paired lobes.

Winged Sumac or **Shining Sumac**
Rhus copallina is a shrub or small tree with compound leaves and 11 to 23 narrow, entire, shiny leaflets, with a midrib bordered by thin "wings". Flowers are clusters of greenish-white blossoms. Fruit is a cluster of red, hairy berries that remain on the plant throughout the winter providing food for wildlife.

Wood Nettle
Laportea canadensis has greenish flowers in loose clusters and the alternate leaves are ovate, petioled and coarsely serrate. The stem has stinging hairs. *L. Canadensis* is similar to *Urtica dioica* (**Stinging Nettle**).

Yellow Mandarin
Disporum lanuginosum is a short plant with horizontal forking branches and alternate leaves. The drooping flower has 6 narrow, greenish-yellow segments with long flaring points.

Yellow Passion Flower

Passiflora lutea is similar to the more common *P. incarnata* but only 1" across and greenish-yellow. The flowers occur in the axils. Leaves are 3-lobed without teeth. A climbing vine with tendrils. Wood edges. Summer to fall.

GLOSSARY OF TERMS USED IN THIS GUIDE

Achene. Dry, one-seeded fruit.
Alien. Foreign, but successfully established.
Alternate. Occurring singly at each node; not opposite.
Auriculate. Having ear-like lobes or appendages.
Axil. The upper angle between the leaf stem and main stalk.
Basal. Pertaining to the base of the plant.
Bract. A modified leaf (in size and shape) usually below the flower.
Calyx. The outer whorl of the perianth.
Cauline. Pertaining to the stem; as opposed to basal.
Cordate. Heart-shaped.
Cleft. Cut deeply toward the base or mid-vein.
Compound. A leaf with two or more leaflets.
Connate. Similar structures that are grown or fused together.
Corolla. The showy inner floral part including petals.
Corymb. A broad flat-topped inflorescence with marginal flowers opening first.
Crenate. Rounded teeth; scalloped.
Cyme. A broad, flat-topped inflorescence with central flowers opening first.
Decumbent. Reclining on the ground with the end ascending.
Disk flower. The tiny tubular flower that forms the round disk in the center of a composite flower.
Elliptic. Broad near the middle and tapering to both ends.
Floret. A small individual flower in the group of flowers.
Glabrous. Without hairs; smooth.
Glaucous. A thin white waxy or powdery covering.
Helical. Coiled or spiral form or structure.
Hirsute. Rough or coarse hair or bristles.
Inflorescence. The flowering part of the plant.
Keel. A ridge; the two anterior united petals of the pea-like flowers.
Lanceolate. Widest below the middle, tapering toward the apex.
Leaflet. The smaller similar parts of a compound leaf.
Linear. Long and narrow with parallel sides.
Lobe. A segment that is projecting.
Obovate. Reversed ovate.
Obcordate. Reversed cordate.
Ocrea. Sheath-like stipule at the node.
Opposite/paired. Occurring in pairs at the same horizontal plane.
Ovate. Egg-shaped; broader below the middle.
Palmate. Divided or lobed radiating from a central point.
Panicle. A multiple inflorescence with racemose branches and pediceled flowers.

Pappus. The hairs, bristles or scales at the tip of the seed.

Parasite. Organism that feeds on another living organism.

Pedicel. Stalk of a single flower that is part of an inflorescence.

Peduncle. The stalk of a flower or a flower cluster.

Perfoliate. When the leaf encircles the stem.

Perianth. The corolla and calyx.

Petiole. The leaf stem.

Pinnate. Arranged on both sides of an axis.

Pinnatifid. Cut to the midrib, appearing pinnately compound.

Pistil. The central reproductive organ of a flower that produces seeds.

Pith. The soft sponge-like tissue in the core of some stems.

Prostrate. Lying flat on the ground.

Pubescent. Hairy.

Raceme. A cluster of flowers arranged singly along a stem, each having its own stalk.

Ray flower. The flat blades that encircle the disk flowers of a composite flower.

Saprophyte. Organism that feeds off a dead organism.

Scabrous. Rough to the touch.

Sepal. A single segment of a divided calyx; usually green.

Serrate. Saw-toothed.

Sessile. Attached directly without any type of stalk.

Simple. A single leaf per stem (petiole).

Spadix. A spike-like structure with embedded flower.

Spathe. A large bract enclosing a flower.

Spike. A flower cluster arranged along a stem singly with stalkless flowers.

Spur. A hollow, tubular extension on a flower.

Stamen. The pollen-bearing organ.

Standard. The upper expanded petal of the pea-like flower.

Stigma. The top of the pistil that receives the pollen.

Stipule. An appendage at the base of a leaf stem.

Style. The narrow tube-like part of the pistil between the ovary and the stigma.

Taproot. Enlarged primary root; sometimes fleshy and edible.

Tendril. A slender threadlike twining organ.

Trichome. Hair-like or bristle structure.

Umbel. Flower cluster with all flower stalks radiating from the same point; umbrella-like.

Whorl. Three or more leaves in a circle; at one node.

Wing. A thin, flat, lateral extension, as the lateral petal in the bean family.

COMPLETE FLOWER

COMPOSITE FLOWER

LEAF SHAPES

Acicular

Cleft or Dissected

Cordate

Deltoid

Elliptic

Filiform

Hastate

Lanceolate

Linear

Lobed

LEAF SHAPES (Continued)

Oblanceolate Obovate Orbicular Oval

Ovate Pinnatifid Reniform Rhombic

Sagittate Spatulate Trullate

LEAF MARGINS

LEAF ATTACHMENTS

LEAF TYPES

Simple

Trifoliate Compound

Palmately Compound

Pinnately Compound

Bipinnately Compound

LEAF ARRANGEMENTS

Alternate

Opposite

Whorled

LEAF VENATION

Arcuate

Net

Parallel

Pinnate

FAMILIES OF FLOWERS IN THIS GUIDE

COMMON FAMILY NAME	FAMILY	SELECTED EXAMPLES FOUND IN THIS GUIDE
Acanthus Family	*Acanthaceae*	Ruellias
Amaranth Family	*Amaranthaceae*	Thorny Pigweed
Arum Family	*Araceae*	Jack-in-the-Pulpit, Green Dragon
Barberry Family	*Berberidaceae*	May-apple, Twinleaf, Blue Cohosh
Bedstraw Family	*Rubiaceae*	Partridge Berry, White Wild Licorice, Bluets
Bignonia Family	*Bignoniaceae*	Trumpet Creeper, Crossvine
Bluebell Family	*Campanulaceae*	Venus' Looking Glass, Southern Harebell, Lobelias, Tall Bellflower
Broomrape Family	*Orobanchaceae*	Squawroot
Buckwheat Family	*Polygonaceae*	Smartweeds, Docks
Buttercup Family	*Ranunculaceae*	Virgin's Bower, Black Cohosh, Thimbleweed, Sharp-Lobed Hepatica, Baneberry, Rue Anemone
Carrot Family	*Apiaceae*	Wild Carrot, Angelica, Sweet Cicely
Composite Family	*Asteraceae*	Ragweed, Goldenrods, Sunflowers, Thistles, Thoroughworts, Ragworts, Asters, Daisies, Yarrow, Horseweed, Boneset
Daffodil Family	*Amaryllidaceae*	Stargrass
Dogbane Family	*Apocynaceae*	Bluestar, Indian Hemp, Periwinkle
Evening-Primrose Family	*Onagraceae*	Showy Evening-Primrose, Common Evening-Primrose
Forget-Me-Not Family	*Boraginaceae*	Turnsole, Bluebells
Gentian Family	*Gentianaceae*	Rose Pink, Cumberland Rose Gentian
Geranium Family	*Geraniaceae*	Wild Geranium
Heath Family	*Ericaceae*	Mountain Laurel, Wild Azalea, Swamp Honeysuckle, Spotted Wintergreen, Indian Pipe
Honeysuckle Family	*Caprifoliaceae*	Japanese Honeysuckle
Iris Family	*Iridaceae*	Crested Dwarf Iris, Blue-eyed Grass
Lily Family	*Liliaceae*	False Solomon's Seal, Devil's Bit, Yucca, Trout Lily, Star of Bethlehem, Solomon's Seal, Trillium
Meadow-Beauty Family	*Melastomataceae*	Virginia Meadow-Beauty
Milkweed Family	*Asclepiadaceae*	Butterfly Weed, Poke Milkweed
Milkwort Family	*Polygalaceae*	Curtiss' Milkwort, Whorled Milkwort
Mint Family	*Lamiaceae*	Mountain Skullcap, Henbit, Basil, Bergamot, Hoary Mountain Mint, Dead-nettle, Hairy Skullcap

COMMON FAMILY NAME	FAMILY	SELECTED EXAMPLES FOUND IN THIS GUIDE
Morning-Glory Family	*Convolvulaceae*	Wild Potato Vine, Small Red Morning-Glory, Dodder, Small White Morning-Glory
Mustard Family	*Brassicaceae*	Cut-Leaved Toothwort, Poorman's Pepper, Shepherd's Purse
Nettle Family	*Urticaceae*	False Nettle, Wood Nettle
Orchid Family	*Orchidaceae*	Pink Lady's Slipper, Ladies' Tresses, Rattlesnake Plantain
Passion Flower Family	*Passifloraceae*	Passion Flower
Pea Family	*Fabaceae*	Trefoils, Partridge-Pea, Vetches, Clovers
Phlox Family	*Polemoniaceae*	Wild Blue Phlox, Carolina Phlox
Pink Family	*Caryophyllaceae*	Fire Pink, Starry Campion, Chickweeds
Plantain Family	*Plantaginaceae*	English Plantain, Common Plantain
Pokeweed Family	*Phytolaccaceae*	Pokeweed
Poppy Family	*Papaveraceae*	Bloodroot, Dutchman's Breeches, Wood Poppy
Primrose Family	*Primulaceae*	Whorled Loosestrife, Fringed Loosestrife
Purslane Family	*Portulacaceae*	Spring Beauty
Rose Family	*Rosaceae*	Multiflora Rose, Blackberries, Agrimony, Strawberry, Cinquefoils
Saxifrage Family	*Saxifragaceae*	Miterwort, Foamflower
Sedum Family	*Crassulaceae*	Wild Stonecrop
Snapdragon Family	*Scrophulariaceae*	Monkey Flower, Wood Betony, Common Mullein, False Foxglove, Moth Mullein, Beardtongues
Spiderwort Family	*Commelinaceae*	Asiatic Dayflower, Spiderwort
Spurge Family	*Euphorbiaceae*	Flowering Spurge
St. John's-wort Family	*Hypericaceae*	Dwarf St. John's-wort, Common St. John's-wort
Tomato Family	*Solanaceae*	Jimsonweed, Horse Nettle
Touch-Me-Not Family	*Balsaminaceae*	Jewel Weed, Touch-Me-Not
Vervain Family	*Verbenaceae*	White Vervain, Narrow-Leaved Vervain
Violet Family	*Violaceae*	Canada Violet, Common Blue Violet, Birdfoot Violet
Waterleaf Family	*Hydrophyllaceae*	Waterleaf, Phacelia
Wood-Sorrel Family	*Oxalidaceae*	Common Wood-Sorrel

BIBLIOGRAPHY

Carman, Jack B. ***Wildflowers of Tennessee.*** Tullahoma, TN: Highland Rim Press, 2001.

Duncan, Wilbur H. and Marion B. Duncan. ***Wildflowers of the Eastern United States.*** Athens, GA: University of Georgia Press, 1995.

Gleason, Henry A. and Arthur Cronquist. ***Manual of Vascular Plants of Northeastern United States and Adjacent Canada.*** New York, NY: Van Nostrand Reinhold Company, 1963.

Little, Elbert L. ***National Audubon Society Field Guide to North American Trees, Eastern Edition.*** New York, NY: Alfred A. Knopf, Inc., 1980.

Niering, William A. and Nancy C. Olmstead. ***The Audubon Society Field Guide to North American Wildflowers, Eastern Region.*** New York, NY: Alfred A. Knopf, Inc., 1979.

Patrick, Thomas S., James R. Allison and Gregory A. Krakow. ***Protected Plants of Georgia.*** Social Circle, GA: Georgia Department of Natural Resources, 1995.

Peterson, Roger Tory and Margaret McKenny. ***A Field Guide to Wildflowers of Northeastern and North-Central North America.*** Boston, MA: Houghton-Mifflin Company, 1975.

Petrides, George A. ***Eastern Trees.*** Boston, MA: Houghton-Mifflin Company, 1988.

___________ ***A Field Guide to Trees and Shrubs.*** Boston, MA: Houghton-Mifflin Company, 1972.

Radford, Albert E., Harry El. Ahler and C. Ritchie Bell. ***Manual of the Vascular Flora of the Carolinas.*** Chapel Hill, NC: University of North Carolina Press, 1968.

Smith, Richard M. ***Wildflowers of the Southern Mountains.*** Knoxville, TN: The University of Tennessee Press, 1998.

Stupka, Arthur. ***Wildflowers in Color.*** New York, NY: Harper and Row, 1965.

BIOGRAPHICAL NOTES

The author is a graduate of the University of Tennessee at Chattanooga where he was a member of Delta Tau Omega and Beta Beta Beta honor societies. Mr. Clark received research grants for work in paleoecology and modern ecology. He holds a Bachelor of Arts degree in geology and a Master of Education degree in combined sciences with teacher certification in physics, chemistry, biology, geology and mathematics. He taught geology laboratory at the University of Tennessee at Chattanooga. He was a Distinguished Military Graduate and was commissioned as an officer in the United States Army. He is a retired science teacher having taught life science, biology, geology and physical sciences for thirty years in Catoosa County, Georgia schools.

After retirement, he was employed with Jacksonville State University (Jacksonville, Alabama) in field archaeology and is presently a volunteer with the Georgia Department of Natural Resources (DNR) working on various wildlife habitat management projects. He is a member of the Georgia Botanical Society, the Georgia Native Plant Society, the Walker County Historical Society and the Central States Archeological Society. He is also a member of the Georgia Wildlife Federation, an affiliate of the National Wildlife Federation.

The author works with DNR in tracking protected plants of northwest Georgia. He also acts as the local steward for the Georgia Botanical Gardens in monitoring plant propagation projects. Mr. Clark is a naturalist with a lifelong interest in all sciences, especially botany and geology. He lives on the lower slopes of Pigeon Mountain in northwest Georgia.

SHIRLEY MILLER WILDFLOWER TRAIL

CROCKFORD-PIGEON MOUNTAIN WILDLIFE MANAGEMENT AREA

A checklist of many of the wildflowers, trees and shrubs
found at the Shirley Miller Wildflower Trail,
a Georgia State Natural Area maintained by the Department of Natural Resources.

WILDFLOWERS

Aniseroot *Osmorhiza longistylis*

Bloodroot *Sanguinaria Canadensis*

Blue Cohosh *Caulophyllum thalictroides*

Bluebells *Mertensia virginica*

Canada Violet *Viola canadensis*

Carolina Phlox *Phlox carolina*

Cleavers *Gallium asprellum*

Columbine *Aquilegia canadensis*

Common Blue Violet *Viola sororia*

Crossvine *Bignonia capreolata*

Cut-leaved Toothwort *Cardamine concatenata*

Dutchman's Breeches *Dicentra cucullaria*

False Solomon's Seal *Smilacina racemosa*

Foamflower *Tiarella cordifolia*

Four-leaved Milkweed *Asclepias quadrifolia*

Geranium *Geranium maculatum*

Great Indian Plantain *Arnoglossum muhlenbergii*

Harbinger of Spring *Erigenia bulbosa*

Hooked Buttercup *Ranunculus recurvatus*

Jack-in-the-Pulpit *Arisaema triphyllum*

Long-spurred Violet *Viola rostrata*

May Apple *Podophyllum peltatum*

Miterwort *Mitella diphylla*

Perfoliate Bellwort *Uvularia perfoliata*

Purple Phacelia *Phacelia bipinnatifida*

Rue Anemone *Thalictrum thalictroides*

Sharp-lobed Hepatica *Hepatica acutiloba*

Slender Toothwort *Dentaria heterophylla*

Solomon's Seal *Polygonatum biflorum*

Spring Beauty *Claytonia caroliniana*

Star Chickweed *Stellaria pubera*

Toadshade *Trillium cuneatum*

Trailing Trillium *Trillium decumbens*

Trout Lily *Erythronium americanum*

Trumpet Creeper *Campsis radicans*

Water Leaf *Hydrophyllum canadense*

White Baneberry *Actaea pachypoda*

White Trillium *Trillium flexipes*

Wild Blue Phlox *Phlox divaricata*

Wild Hyacinth *Camassia scilloides*

Wild Stonecrop *Sedum ternatum*

Wood Betony *Pedicularis canadensis*

Wood Nettle *Laportea canadensis*

Wood Poppy *Stylophorum diphyllum*

Yellow Mandarin *Disporum lanuginosum*

TREES

American Hornbeam *Carpinus caroliniana*

Beech *Fagus grandifolia*

Black Locust *Robinia pseudoacacia*

Black Walnut *Juglans nigra*

Box Elder *Acer negundo*

Eastern Hophornbeam *Ostrya virginiana*

Hackberry *Celtis occidentalis*

Ohio Buckeye *Aesculus glabra*

Sugar Maple *Acer saccharum*

Sweetgum *Liquidamber styraciflua*

Sycamore *Platanus occidentalis*

Tulip Poplar *Liriodendron tulipifera*

White Basswood *Tilia heterophylla*

Yellow Buckeye *Aesculus octandra*

Yellowwood *Cladrastis kentukea*

SHRUBS

American Bladdernut *Staphylea trifolia*

PawPaw *Asimina triloba*

Spicebush *Lindera benzoin*

INDEX

V.

W.

Y.

Z.

NOTES